LET THE CHILDREN COME . . . TO COMMUNION

Stephen Lake

T0324308

First published in Great Britain in 2006

Society for Promoting Christian Knowledge
36 Causton Street
London SW1P 4ST

British Library Cataloguing-in-Publication Data
A catalogue record for this book is available from the British Library

ISBN-13: 978–0–281–05795–5
ISBN-10: 0–281–05795–8

1 3 5 7 9 10 8 6 4 2

Typeset by Graphicraft Ltd, Hong Kong
Printed in Great Britain by Ashford Colour Press

Then little children were being brought to him in order that he might lay his hands on them and pray. The disciples spoke sternly to those who brought them; but Jesus said, 'Let the little children come to me, and do not stop them; for it is to such as these that the kingdom of heaven belongs.'

Matthew 19.13–14

*To my father and mother,
David and Heather.
Thank you.*

Contents

Author's note

Admission of the Baptised to Communion

This new liturgy can be used or adapted for the admission of baptized children to Holy Communion. It can be found in *Christian Initiation*, © The Archbishops' Council 2006, ISBN 0–7151–2102–2, pages 188–92.

Foreword

For a steadily growing number of local Anglican communities, the admission of children to Holy Communion is becoming a central part of their mission strategy. It is a practice that affirms the seriousness with which the Church takes its younger members (*not* 'the Church of the future', as the hackneyed phrase goes, but an intrinsic element in the Church of the present). It takes it for granted that children need as believers what adults need – nurture, listening, stretching of the mind and heart. It moves decisively away from the deeply rooted assumption that adolescence is the best moment to make the transition into full visible participation in the sacramental life of the Church – a rather questionable presupposition at the best of times; and so it offers some viable alternative to the 'Confirmation as passing-out parade' model which is the sad reality in many places.

Slowly, the Church of England has been learning (not least, learning *from* its younger members) that it is a community for all, not only the elderly, or for the articulate, or for the 'mature' – not even just for the teenagers. This excellent book helps us trace some of this story in the life of our Church. It introduces us to a wide range of good practice and careful reflection from prominent teachers and leaders. It gives the rationale in our theology for the practice. And, not least, it offers simple and practical advice: 'Don't panic!' is its message to clergy and lay leaders – there are all kinds of ways of handling the problems that you foresee, and others have been there before. If there are risks, they are worth taking for the sake of really sharing Christ's life in his Body with the children whose company he loved on earth and loves still.

Stephen Lake has written a fine, timely guide to current discussion. I hope his vision will invite and persuade, and that we shall as a Church continue to discover the riches that await us as we listen more thoughtfully and generously to Christ's youngest friends.

+ *Rowan Cantuar:*

Introduction

We are told that the Christian life is a journey. For parents of little children, this has another meaning. After frantically packing the car for two hours, remembering to water the plants and finally feeding the goldfish (remember what you came back to last year!) it is time to set off for the dreaded motorway journey. Four minutes into the three-hour run comes the immortal phrase from the back seat: 'Are we nearly there yet?'

Children have little awareness of travelling times or the stress of preparing for the journey but they do travel with us and have a unique and dynamic understanding of God's love. Children are equal members of the church by virtue of their baptism and therefore should have full access to the sacraments, the signs of God's love, and most especially to the bread and the wine of the Eucharist.

Nearly ten years ago, the General Synod approved the Guidelines for the Admission of Baptised Children to Holy Communion. Since then, only 10 per cent of parishes have taken this up, yet those that have done so have found this development to be fundamental to their growth and mission.

The aim of this book is to:

- encourage the admission of baptized children to communion;
- summarize in one place relevant practice, information and theology; and
- move the debate on, encouraging the Church into full participation.

It will provide enough information and background to serve as a parish resource for those places wishing and needing to develop ministry in this way. This is an attempt to be both accessible and anecdotal, rooted in the realities of getting things done in parishes. So this is not meant to be the last theological word on the subject but an encouragement into action.

Like many others, some time ago I became aware of the importance of this opening up of the Eucharist to all the baptized, regardless of age. I was involved in introducing this practice to my last post, which became a thriving urban congregation, and also introducing it across Salisbury Diocese with its rich mix of urban, suburban and rural parishes. Later came the challenge of leading the introduction of children and communion in a cathedral community and advising others on how to go about this exciting rediscovery.

People often say that children are the church of the future. This is wrong. Children belong to the church of today, but will be adults in the church of tomorrow. How children experience their membership of the church now will form their participation in the church in the future.

Jesus had a special love for children, and had to teach the disciples to let them come to him. As we approach ten years of wide experience in the life of the Church of children receiving our Lord in the bread and the wine, they have the right to ask us all, 'Are we nearly there yet?'

Stephen Lake

1

Coming of age

Children and the tradition of the Church

It is nearly ten years since the General Synod of the Church of England approved Guidelines, produced by the House of Bishops, for the Admission of Baptised Persons to Holy Communion before Confirmation. In the following decade, significant growth has taken place across the whole Church. In July 2005, following another Synod debate, the *Church Times* headline read, 'Admitting children to communion is gaining ground'.

The ten-year-old member of the church

A child born ten years ago will now be coming of age in the life of the church. As well as being towards the top end of primary school and preparing for the coming year's change to secondary school, a ten-year-old will be on the verge of many things. Double figures are a milestone for all children as they become more self-aware, less shy, experiencing more freedom at home and when out at play. Sleep-overs begin to creep in (I've yet to discover where the 'sleep' bit comes in) and there is a growing interest in television and films beyond kids' TV after 3pm. Bedtime is creeping later and toys are fine so long as they can be plugged into the National Grid. Brownies become Guides, Cubs become Scouts and Dad is now a total embarrassment.

If this ten-year-old goes to church, he or she will be approaching the minimum age for confirmation in the diocese. The ten-year-old may have started serving at the altar and is known by lots of adults as a person, by name. Here adults are also known by their Christian names. The ten-year-old is at the top of Sunday School and looking forward to the more exciting-looking youth club which meets on a Friday evening in the church hall. There are lots of friends in church and the parish priest always says hello. Each Sunday, everyone receives Holy Communion, everyone. This ten-year-old belongs here.

This parish began admitting children to communion soon after the Synod decision. The Diocesan Children's Adviser came to speak to the PCC and, after much careful preparation, children started taking the bread and the wine. It felt right, it felt natural; many wondered why they hadn't done this before. Over time, the whole understanding of the parish changed as nurture became a life-long experience and growth became a norm. The ten-year-old child feels included, equal, valued and, as he/she stands on the verge of many changes and personal choices, more a part of the whole as this is what Christians do.

The forty-year-old member of the church

It's actually almost forty years since the Church of England started discussing this matter. In that time, several generations have grown up, prevented from the sacrament of Holy Communion until and only if they have been confirmed. While this is a clear and structured way of affirming membership, indeed the inherited Anglican norm, alone it is not the whole story. A forty-year-old may well have grown up in the life of the church, similarly to our ten-year-old, but so much of church seemed to be about jumping through hoops rather than unconditional belonging. Growing in searching, the forty-year-old believes that Jesus is about unconditional love, but as there was nothing to keep him/her at church when a child, little sense or sign of real belonging, he/she drifted away. Occasional attendance at Christmas and Easter seems to assuage the conscience, yet strangely he/she always receives communion at Midnight

Mass, as everybody does, and no-one seems to mind or ask any questions. Returning to worship is a challenging prospect, and it would be good if there was a way in, a sense of welcome, not just from the people, who all seem nice, but from God himself. If only . . .

Growing up

These are rather unfair characterizations but they seek to summarize the situation we, as a Church, have found ourselves in. There has been a growing awareness, both theologically and liturgically, that the Church has needed to listen to the Spirit in moving away from a rather formal approach to membership to allow for a more definitive and creative insight to the importance of Holy Baptism as the sign of membership of the Church, from which naturally flows the unique meal of membership. The outward and visible sign of being a member of the Body of Christ is receiving Holy Communion, regularly, bestowing as it does the inward and spiritual gift of Christ himself. This is not, and should not be, bounded by age. We are called to let the children come.

Movements of the Spirit can take a while when the third person of the Trinity has to work through us and our delightful human structures, but, like our ten-year-old who has been nurtured and our forty-year-old who wants to return, we may now be coming of age. No-one will suggest that the admission of all the baptized to Holy Communion is the answer to all the Church's concerns, but how can we address such concerns in church life and, more importantly, in the world if we have a mistaken view of our own membership? The Church of England must grasp this movement of the Spirit with the enthusiasm of a child and the maturity of an adult so that we are as whole as we can be as the Kingdom of God comes of age.

The infancy of the Church

The earliest Christians called their faith 'The Way', as a response to their understanding of living in a new way and being on a journey of faith. The journey included everybody; children were present in the earliest Christian communities and were initiated into the faith along with adults. So for children, as for anyone else, membership of the Church is obtained by baptism and thereafter depends on continuing participation in the Eucharist.

For this reason, although there is no explicit mention of children sharing in the Eucharist in the New Testament, they would have been both present and participants. Families and households were baptized and initiated into the faith together (Colossians 3 and Ephesians 5). In addition, the Jewish Passover tradition, which would have had a strong influence on the Eucharistic sharing, gave children a central role in the ritual. Children were given a place of honour at the Passover meal and often led adults in reliving the Passover experience. Jesus himself would have been familiar with this role. By implication, therefore, children were indeed receiving communion from the earliest times of our faith, sharing the worship with adults, mostly in their homes.

Likewise, there is no explicit evidence in the post-apostolic era to suggest that children receiving communion was abnormal or problematic. Infant baptism and communion were well established in Carthage by the time of Cyprian (d. 259), whose writings describe infants receiving bread and wine from birth. The Apostolic Constitutions from fourth-century Syria, without being age specific, provide that children receive communion after the clergy, widows and deaconesses, but before the main body of adults. Augustine of Hippo was the first to make the link between baptism and participation in heaven through the doctrine of Original Sin. 'Unless you eat the flesh of the Son of Man and drink his blood, you have no life in you' (John

6.53). This was a key text for Augustine. To deny children baptism by reason of age or lack of understanding was to deny them Christ himself in the form of bread and wine, which in turn denies them a place in heavenly peace. Infants should therefore be baptized as soon as possible, and receive the signs of the membership and participation given in being in Christ.

From this almost obvious and natural understanding of the place of children in the Christian community, developments came as the Church grew in size and complexity. The role of the bishop had always been central to Christian initiation; he was the president of the unified rite of Baptism, Confirmation and Eucharist. Dioceses grew up with greater distances involved and greater numbers to be baptized. In time, the water rite and signing of the cross was increasingly delegated to presbyters and the laying on of hands reserved for the now less frequent visit of the bishop. From these beginnings we can see the place of confirmation, but admission to communion was still given from the point of baptism.

This is still the case in the Orthodox churches of the East where infant communion is the norm, immediately following baptism. In the East the right and need of children to receive communion remains unquestioned and they communicate infrequently, like the adults, and on equal terms with them.

Changes in the West

Regular receiving of communion, attendance at Mass and the heightened importance of the consecrated elements combined together to decrease participation in the eucharistic meal for the laity. The clericalization of the Church in the West led to the need for great care to be taken with the 'real' presence of Jesus in the consecrated elements and subsequently, either by design or default, the laity were often denied the wine and given only bread, while children were sometimes denied altogether. In 1281, Archbishop Peckham at the Council of Lambeth issued the regulation that those not confirmed (without good reason) should be barred from communion. This was an attempt to counter the 'damnable negligence' of parents who failed to present their children to the bishop for the laying on of hands. While the concern was indeed for those not receiving communion, the increased emphasis on the 'confirmation' moment was gaining ground. The practice of communicating unconfirmed adults and children was finally abolished by the Council of Trent in the sixteenth century.

The emphasis brought by the Reformation also discouraged children from taking communion. For valuable reasons instruction and understanding were give high priority, but this brought the receiving of communion much more into the adults-only world. Cranmer's Prayer Book of 1549 stated that 'there shall none be admitted to the Holy Communion, until such time as he can say the catechism, and be confirmed'. The key here is the order of things, the learning of the catechism a prerequisite. However, at the Savoy Conference in 1661 it was agreed that those 'ready and desirous to be confirmed' could receive communion. The Prayer Book of 1662 enshrined the compromise: 'And there shall none be admitted to the Holy Communion until such time as he be confirmed or ready and desirous to be confirmed.' Thereafter, Anglican communicants were adults or older young people who were admitted to communion on the basis of being baptized and having received some sort of instruction from the parish priest. Bishops came to confirm at varying intervals.

In the nineteenth century confirmation was administered much more rigorously and developed as a precondition to receiving communion. The pattern of Baptism followed much later by Confirmation and Communion, which is familiar to most members of the Church of England, is therefore at best a variation of the early tradition and practice and, at worst, a departure from the Christian norm. It may be what we are familiar with but that does not mean the Spirit cannot lead us into a new understanding. The 'passing out parade' has become all too familiar. The Roman Catholic Church continues to offer First Communion to children from around the age of seven years old.

The Parish Communion Movement of the twentieth century, to a large extent, sought to recover the importance of children participating in the Eucharistic celebration. Children were welcomed into the main Sunday morning service with a new enthusiasm, especially as Sunday Schools shifted from afternoon meeting times to Sunday mornings. Children went first to Sunday School and then joined the service, often in time for the distribution of communion, although not able to receive themselves. As the liturgy of the Church began to include children in new and real ways, it became more and more obvious that their exclusion from the meal shared by adults was literally that, exclusive. Children came forward to the communion rail for a blessing, a lovely moment but a second best to receiving Holy Communion. The participation and increased status of children at the Parish Eucharist has brought into sharp focus the right and need for children to share in the whole celebration.

In their book *Children, Churches and Christian Learning*, Leslie J. Francis and Jeff Astley[1] summarize the factors that, over this period of time, have come together to stimulate the debate and process towards admitting children to communion. These factors are:

- the more central place of communion in the local church;
- the move toward fuller participation by children in worship;
- fresh discussion on the pattern of Christian initiation;
- new understandings of how faith develops;
- growing emphasis on the Church as community;
- fresh insights as to how children learn by participation;
- demands both from children and parents for fuller participation;

- recognition of changing practices ecumenically and internationally.

Time to report

The General Synod of the Church of England discussed children and communion in July 2005. In *Children and Holy Communion: a Review* (GS 1576), a summary of the position we have found ourselves in read as follows:

> Since the 1950s, there has been a growing theological awareness of baptism as the one complete rite of initiation. Baptised children are wholly, not conditionally, in the Body of Christ. There has been a growing sense that they are part of the sacramental community and should, with appropriate nurture and support, be welcomed at the communion rail with adults. The process of the consideration of this issue began some 60 years ago, with the growth of Parish Communion as the main service in many churches.[2]

This summary points to the rediscovery of understanding, especially of the importance of baptism, which has been represented in years of reporting and experimentation.

1967 The National Evangelical Congress (Keele) said: 'Some ... would like the children of Christian families to be admitted as communicants at an early age.' The Ely Commission was asked to consider questions about initiation.

1971 The Ely Commission Report is published, *Christian Initiation: Birth and Growth in Christian Society* (CIO 1971). It concluded that Baptism is the complete sacramental initiation rite, therefore children should be admitted to Holy Communion on that basis. General Synod received the Ely Report.

1974 General Synod referred the report to the dioceses for consultation. Three dioceses – Manchester, Peterborough and Southwark – were given permission to admit children on an 'experimental' basis.

1976 General Synod formally decides not to admit children to Holy Communion by a 60/40 majority. However, Manchester, Peterborough and Southwark continue to admit. *The Child in the Church* is published by the British Council of Churches.

1978 The Scottish Episcopal Church agrees to admit to Holy Communion before Confirmation.

1979 The new Episcopal Church of USA Prayer Book offers an ambiguous reading of provisions. Children and infants are admitted to Holy Communion as a result.

1980 New Zealand and South Africa make provision to admit children.

1981 *Understanding Christian Nurture* published by the British Council of Churches. Australia approves provisional canons.

1982 The Faith and Order Commission of the World Council of Churches suggests in the Lima Document: 'Those churches which baptise children but refuse them a share in the Eucharist before such a rite [i.e. confirmation] may wish to ponder whether they have fully appreciated and accepted the consequence of baptism.'

1984 By now most Australian dioceses have adopted the canons.

1985 The Knaresborough Report, *Communion before Confirmation?*, is prepared for the General Synod. It recommends that regulations for the admission of baptized people to Holy Communion should be drawn up and approved. Synod 'takes note' in November but Manchester, Peterborough and Southwark as 'experimental' dioceses are asked to report back. The Joint Board of

Education in Australia publishes *Helping Children to Participate in Holy Communion.*

1988 The major report *Children in the Way* is published and debated in General Synod, which accepts it, including the recommendation 'A resolution of the issue of Communion before Confirmation is required as a matter of urgency.' The matter is passed to the House of Bishops.

1989 *Children and Holy Communion,* an ecumenical report, is published by the British Council of Churches.

1991 *All God's Children?* (GS 988 1991) states that only 15 per cent of children under thirteen years were involved in church-related activities. It questions whether Sunday is the best day on which to reach un-churched children and urges parishes to explore other means through schools and the wider community.

1993 *Communion before Confirmation.* The Culham College Institute is commissioned to do a survey of the three experimental dioceses. A survey conducted by the Children's Advisers finds experimentation is happening in all dioceses.

1994 *On the Way – Towards an Integrated Approach to Christian Initiation,* a report of General Synod, asks churches to explore initiation policies. One of the options for consideration is Communion before Confirmation.

1996 The House of Bishops produces Guidelines for Admission of Baptised Persons to Holy Communion before Confirmation (July). General Synod accepts the Guidelines (November).

1997 The House of Bishops' Guidelines are published in March, with minor amendments.

This (adapted) summary above from GS 1576 concludes:

The Guidelines permitted and encouraged churches to explore the nature of the sacrament and the question of who should receive, including children. Just as with adults, the spiritual life of baptised children is enriched by the receiving of Holy Communion and their sense of belonging is affirmed and encouraged. This has required churches to engage with the sacrament in new and different ways, to the enrichment of both children and adults alike, as they journey in faith together.[3]

Finally, in 1997, the book *Children and Holy Communion* by Steve Pearce and Diana Murrie gave a useful overview of the history and background of this whole area and offered a course for the preparation of candidates. This work became the standard text for most parishes entering this whole area for the first time. It was republished in 2004. Murrie and Pearce gather all the changes and reports into this statement:

> The convincing arguments in favour of a change in practice seem to have been,
>
> • the nature of baptism
> • the acceptance of children in the church
> • children's need for spiritual nourishment
> • children's need to belong
> • the need for adults to 'become as a child'.
>
> The House of Bishops address the nature of baptism in these terms: 'The entire profession of the Christian life . . . is represented in the action of baptism' . . . In other words, baptism makes us full members of the Body of Christ.[4]

Way-mark reports

The process described above was long but creative. Most decisive among the many reports and consultations were two particular documents which formed the Church's thinking in new and important directions. Both hark back, in their titles, to those early Christians who saw all ages as being part of 'The Way'.

Children in the Way was a report by the General Synod Board of Education. Its subtitle was 'New directions for the Church's children'. The new direction was to put children on an equal footing with others in the life of the Church. The traditional Sunday School pattern was creaking and a new all-age, all-stage vision was proclaimed. The concept of 'the journey of faith' was acknowledged and valued, challenging not only General Synod but parishes and individuals to review the development of faith and understanding. The title, *Children in the Way*, could be read two ways – this was deliberate. Too many churches were happy with children so long as they were seen and not heard, literally 'in the way'; but the only way 'to be in' was The Way of faith and nurture. The Introduction set this principle out clearly:

> Our conviction is simple. If children are to continue in the way of faith, if they are to continue on the path to which the Church welcomed them at baptism, then they must be aided and supported by the adult fellow-Christians who are also on that journey and must be acknowledged as those who sometimes lead the way. We invite you to join us in searching for new strategies and models for Christian education in parishes, in order that both adults and children may journey together in the way of Christ, growing into his full stature and serving his world.[5]

The report began by describing childhood and the modern influences on children. With numbers of children attending traditional models of nurture declining, evangelism among children was a priority. Different models of children's work were examined and the 'pilgrim' model of church encouraged. A major survey was detailed to ascertain the range and effectiveness of the current provision for children. The report was taken up by deaneries and parishes with enthusiasm as it gave a clear lead for renewal and development in children's work. A change in mindset was achieved, as churches realized that the future direction was in promoting an all-age outlook. Seventeen recommendations were made, many of them rooted in practicality and aimed at each and every PCC.

One of the recommendations was: 'A resolution of the issue of Communion before Confirmation is required as a matter of urgency' (Chapter 4, Recommendation 2).

ON the WAY: Towards an Integrated Approach to Christian Initiation was a theologically profound report blessed by the work of the late Michael Vasey, then of St John's College, Durham, to whom the Church of England owes a significant debt. Published half way through the Decade of Evangelism, the report saw the welcome and nurture of new Christians as one of the most important tasks facing the Christian community. The report stated that at least three patterns of Christian initiation existed in the Church of England and suggested that the catechumenate model could be a hopeful and positive framework in which to exercise this multiplicity of faith journey, story and growth. Careful attention was given throughout the report to the practice of the early church and of other denominations.

Chapter 5 concentrated on The Initiation of Children, even though the heart of the report was based on an adult catechumenate. It said: 'The practice of infant baptism, baptismal theologies that emphasise grace or covenant, and contemporary educational theories, all point to the same conclusion: the experience of belonging is the basis for nurture and growth in the Christian life.'[6]

To move to the admission of children to communion from a young age, if not from baptism itself, would be consistent with Christian practice in the first millennium of the Church and the continuing practice of the Orthodox. It was acknowledged that the Church of England had already come close to agreeing this in principle but had found it difficult to find a way of acting upon this consensus. Questions and difficulties were examined in detail and taken seriously. Likewise, the implications for the various initiation patterns, if children were to be admitted to communion, and the impact on other Christian churches, were debated. In summary, the report could see the imperative for a change in practice but any such change needed to be aware of the variety of initiation patterns in use and the real need, if a catechumenate approach is to be used, that on-going, organic faith development should be in place and in use. The report backed this up by quoting the 1991 Toronto Consultation which affirmed the statement 'Children and Communion' of the First Anglican Liturgical Consultation in 1985: 'that since baptism is the sacramental sign of full incorporation into the church, all baptized persons be admitted to communion'. *ON the WAY* goes on to affirm this in its context: 'Catechumenal approaches emphasise the different dimensions of Christian initiation and rightly urge their more effective integration with sacramental practice. What is being asserted is that full sacramental initiation is the proper precondition for the nurture of children growing up in the life of the Church.'[7]

If *Children in the Way* changed the Church's mindset regarding children, *ON the WAY* helped the Church understand more fully the importance of on-going faith development and of proper sacramental and liturgical expression of that faith, at whatever age or stage. The whole process of change, and in particular the work contained in these documents, finally saw the Church of England 'coming of age' in its understanding of the place of children in relation to Holy Communion. It was just as well, for as the British Council of Churches report *The Child in the Church* put it:

> The Church that does not accept children unconditionally in its fellowship is depriving those children of what is rightfully theirs, but the deprivation such as the Church itself will suffer is far more grave.[8]

14

Notes

1 Leslie J. Francis and Jeff Astley, *Children, Churches and Christian Learning* (SPCK, 2002), p. 29.
2 *Children and Holy Communion: a Review* (GS 1576).
3 *Children and Holy Communion: a Review.*
4 Diana Murrie and Steve Pearce, *Children and Holy Communion* (National Society/Church House Publishing, 1997), p. 3.
5 *Children in the Way* (National Society/Church House Publishing, 1988), Introduction p. 1, Recommendation 2 p. 91.
6 *ON the WAY* (GS Misc 444 Church House Publishing, 1995), p. 92.
7 *ON the WAY*, p. 93.
8 *The Child in the Church: Reports of the Working Parties on 'The Child in the Church' and 'Understanding Christian Nurture'* (British Council of Churches, 1976).

2

Out of the mouths of babes

Children in the Bible

As will become very obvious, the author is no biblical scholar. In this chapter I do not provide a full exegesis of the place of children in scripture, but as before I try to give an accessible way into the subject, to provide an overview that will encourage further study and action. It is more likely that the texts discussed here will provide a springboard for preaching or work in groups. The task is two-fold, to ensure that there is nothing biblical that rules out the giving of communion to children before a rite such as confirmation, and then to find, however implicit, the biblical picture of God's revelation to us, and in particular to children.

Children in the Old Testament

Throughout the Old Testament, children are seen as a gift from God and a sign of the covenant relationship with him. Lineage is secured by the gift of children; the future of God's people is in the provision of an heir. Even at the very beginning of scripture, this pivotal place of children is assumed and verified. Adam and Eve are commissioned to 'Be fruitful and multiply' (Genesis 1.28), children being required for the continuance of God's creation. In Genesis chapter 4, Cain is conceived and born 'with the help of the Lord'. Even though this first family becomes somewhat dysfunctional, God is fully involved in both the provision of children and their development.

The place of children therefore in the Jewish nation is so established and rooted that it does not need to be separately identified or explained. Children are part of the family, the family being the archetypal Jewish religious community. They are involved in the ritual that expresses the Jewish identity: 'And when your children ask you, "What do you mean by this observance?", you shall say, "It is the Passover sacrifice to the Lord, for he passed over the houses of the Israelites in Egypt, when he struck down the Egyptians but spared our houses"' (Exodus 12.26–27).

Children would then also have been seen as part of the covenant relationship with God that made the Jewish people unique. Male children became part of the faith community through the ritual of circumcision, often only a few days after birth. In modern Judaism, bar mitzvah, around the ages of twelve or thirteen, is the act of a boy taking personal responsibility to fulfil the Torah for himself within the community. (Overtones of Christian infant baptism followed by more mature confirmation are obvious.) But all through the intervening years, male children by circumcision and female children by membership of the family are part of the dynamic Covenant relationship with God of election, worship, estrangement and renewal. Children are part of the family, the faith community, and are the hope of the future. They are not second-class; they are part of the whole. Two major Old Testament stories illustrate these points.

Abraham and Isaac

It is probably true that we are all familiar with the many Bible accounts that contain children, but so often we remember them for the role and influence of the adult involved rather than that of the child. The dramatic and somewhat frightening account of the testing of Abraham and the near sacrifice of his long-awaited son Isaac is a case in point. God appeared to Abram (as he was called then in Chapter 17) to establish the Everlasting Covenant. Abram was to become Abraham and, despite his increasing years and the age of his wife (now called Sarah), he would receive a son to be called Isaac (Genesis 17.18). The child, not born until Chapter 21, is duly named Isaac and circumcised at eight days old. Isaac is the sign of the covenant relationship.

But in Chapter 22 God tests Abraham. He commands him to take Isaac to Mount Moriah to sacrifice the boy as an offering to the Lord. They get up early the next morning and, with everything prepared, travel to their destination. The boy is no fool and asks his father where the animal for the sacrifice is. Abraham's words of reply are as much evasion of the truth, to protect the child, as a confession of faith. When the time comes to sacrifice the boy, the same boy who was prepared to speak up and ask his father an awkward question is silent as he is prepared to be killed. Either Abraham binds his mouth (although any child of mine would have had something to say about this activity), or his words are simply not recorded, or he is presented as being in tune with God's will and accepting of the consequences of his father's actions. There is also no account of complaining afterwards! Of course, the point of the account is to test Abraham's faith by placing in jeopardy not just his son but the child of the promise, the one upon whom all the hopes of the future depend. This is crucial; the whole deck of cards could fall at this point, quite apart from the killing of a child. Isaac is both questioning at the beginning to show he is engaged as part of the covenant relationship, and silent in his acceptance that he must be part of God's plan. He is innocent and there is no way that God is going to allow him to die, despite the obedience of Abraham: 'Do not lay your hand on the boy or do anything to him' (v. 12). In this account, a child is both the subject of hope, the symbol of obedience and sacred to God.

In the New Testament, Isaac is referred to in Galatians 4.22–31, prefiguring Christians as children of promise. In Hebrews 11.17–19 the sacrifice of Isaac is seen both as an example of faith and as a prefiguring of the Passion. In Christian art, illustrations of this account have always been used as a figure of the Eucharist. The child Isaac has more meaning to him than first meets the reader's eye.

Samuel and Eli

This has to be one of my favourite Bible stories, I suppose for two reasons: first because this time it is the boy who is the focus, and secondly because I have a son called Samuel. Sam suffers the perennial clergy kid problem of never being picked for anything during a school assembly because Mum or Dad is taking the act of worship. He would always put his hand up but I would choose others to answer so as not to show any favouritism. But once in school we were looking at 1 Samuel 2.18ff. and how to respond to God's call, and so I could only choose him for our little play. As the account was read, I was old Eli and he was the boy Samuel, on a camp bed, in front of the whole school, leaping up and down as a sign of obedience. The assembly worked well and it was natural to use the only Samuel in the school. I can't read this passage without thinking of that day. It reminds us how, when an infant, Sam would never sleep and how he gave us such long nights. Now the problem is getting him out of bed at all.

According to Jewish tradition Samuel was about twelve years old at this time; the age Jesus was when he spoke with the teachers in the Temple at Jerusalem. This story must have been in the mind of St Luke when he wrote his Gospel. Samuel was dedicated to the Lord and was a model of faithfulness. 'Now the boy Samuel continued to grow both in stature and in favour with the Lord and with the people' (v. 26). While the boy was about his business, serving the Lord under Eli, God called him to be a contrasting figure to the sons of Eli who might normally be expected to follow in their father's footsteps. Samuel is an example of growing spirituality and openness to the Lord God. Three times he is called by God, replying with the innocent 'Here I am.' He runs to Eli thinking that Eli is calling but it is not him. Finally the older man helps the child by instructing him in the correct response so that when God, who will not let go, calls him again, he can say the right thing. God does call, Samuel dutifully responds and the news is not good. The poor child lies there until morning before being quizzed by Eli and Samuel passes on God's judgement. Samuel, again in contrast, continues to grow and flourish, becoming in time the premier prophet in Israel.

The boy Samuel in this account is the mouthpiece of God and a symbol of innocent obedience, a model of call and response. He has 'neat' vocation, commitment combined with enthusiasm. God is clearly content to use a child to model faithful response and to be his own messenger.

God and children

Psalm 8 is a hymn that celebrates God's glory and the God-given dignity of human beings. Included among those with this dignity are babes and infants. This well-known phrase, 'Out of the mouths of babes', is used in common conversation to make the point that the truth can come from unexpected quarters, especially the youngest, most innocent, members of society. So children are not secondary figures in the divine plan, and indeed throughout the Old Testament this is made clear. Children are regarded as divine gifts (Genesis 4.1; 33.5), pledges of God's favour and the heritage of the Lord (Psalm 127.3).

All through the Old Testament there is this reverence for the gift of children and a tenderness towards the life of each child. There is an appreciation of the simplicity offered by the young and affection for their openness and honesty. This is the basis for Jesus' treatment of children.

God chooses certain children, like Samuel, to be the first beneficiaries and messengers of his revelation. David is singled out in preference to his older brothers (1 Samuel 16.1–13) and the young David continually shows himself to be wiser than the leaders of his day. The high point of references to the child is the messianic prophesy of the birth of Immanuel as told in Isaiah 7.14ff. The royal child is proclaimed who will re-establish justice and herald the Kingdom of God. If God is content to work through the young in this way, then the Church ought to be able to value their place in the community of the faithful by sharing its most wonderful gift with pleasure. Otherwise, they might have something to say from those mouths of theirs!

Bread from heaven

Two texts are often linked and preached on together. They cross the boundary from the Old Testament to the New Testament. Neither is directly about children but both point again to this implicit understanding of children within the worshipping life of the faithful.

Exodus 16 tells of the feeding by God of the people in the wilderness. The people go out to collect this practical and spiritual sustenance as a community; it is not communion but it is for all of them, serving the needs of their hunger and the avoidance of the influence of Egypt. God did not pick which members of the community were to receive this food, it was for all, mirroring the understanding of the people about the inclusion of all in their ritual. Just as all the people crossed the Red Sea, so all the people need to be sustained by God himself. There is no one way for adults and another way for others.

The feeding of the five thousand is the only miracle recorded by all four Gospels. Again it is out of concern (in John 6) for the people's welfare that Jesus raises the question of food, knowing at the same time that such a feeding would have a miraculous and deeply spiritual meaning. The disciples were once again missing the point. It took a boy to be found and to be prepared to share his small resources with so many. There is no argument from the boy. In contrast to the stupidity of the disciples, the boy offers his goods freely and without question. Once again in scripture, it takes a child to leaven the lump.

21

This chapter goes on of course to teach us all that Christ is the true bread from heaven. 'I am the bread of life,' says Jesus. 'Whoever comes to me will never be hungry and whoever believes in me will never be thirsty.' The only criteria for being fed the Bread of Life are: to come and to believe. Children do that just as adults do. In fact, like the boy with the loaves and fishes, they are more likely to be willing and able than many of us ever will be. The rest of Chapter 6 makes this very clear. Surely, it is right for all to say with one voice, 'Sir, give us this bread always.'

Children in the Gospels

One of the best liturgical principles around is that of 'visiting' your own church. By this I mean that we can become so familiar with our beloved surroundings and so busy with the business of life, that often we don't see what is there in front of us all the time. In liturgy, this means that all too often, we worry about text and style before seeing what welcomes or confronts people when they enter a church for the first time. We rarely ask ourselves if a locked door or a fees notice should be the first thing to greet people when they try to cross the threshold, or whether the ancient font near the door ought to stand for something more meaningful and symbolic about baptism and entry into the household of faith, than as a useful receptacle for the flower guild. These symbols of our faith are there but often we don't see them. The same can be true of the Gospel narratives with which we are so familiar. We know them so well but it's easy to take their significance for granted.

For example, when considering the importance of children to God, and their place within the community of faith, we must take seriously the fact that Matthew and Luke deem it important enough to record not just that the Word was made flesh but that the incarnation was vested in a child, an infant, who went on to grow through childhood. It is an inescapable fact that God came to dwell among us first as a child, in fulfilment of his promise. Coming in the form of a child was deliberate and conscious, telling us something about God himself.

The place and importance of children is obvious and explicit. Implications for the place of children within the Christian community are implicit, and therefore need careful reading and understanding. It is important not to load our own cultural enthusiasms onto scriptural text, but how often have you heard a sermon preached about the importance of children to the church? The involvement of children in God's revelation through Jesus is clear; their status thereafter is not so clear or is easily missed – mainly because we are no longer children ourselves. The same is true when we contemplate a theology of childhood: it is usually in passing in relation to another issue, such as abortion. This is inadequate because, while society often asks children to behave like adults, in the Gospel of Jesus Christ we are asked to become like children in order to enter the Kingdom of God.

The child Jesus

Luke 2. 21–40, the Gospel reading for Candlemas (2 Feb), is a powerful all-age account and can be used to bring a whole congregation together with a sense of unity and common commitment. I have used this simple address with good effect a few times and it works with large congregations as well as when there are small numbers present.

Jesus was brought to Jerusalem as an infant for the rite of presentation and purification. St Luke's next account is the parallel story of Jesus coming to Jerusalem for the Passover when he was twelve years old. It is not difficult to begin the address/sermon/talk by rehearsing the details of this beautifully crafted encounter. It's one of those stories that people know and can visualize in their heads as you retell it in your own words. You should not need notes (or the safety of a pulpit) to do this confidently. The new parents bring their pride and joy to the

Lord, just as many parents bring their children for Baptism today. It is one of the first memorable events in the life of a new family. Waiting for them is an old man who is an example of faithfulness and hope in the Lord. He is assisted by an equally interesting female senior citizen, Anna, who speaks to everyone with grandmotherly enthusiasm about this child.

Having set the scene, ask the congregation for a volunteer. Who here today is the oldest person in church? Ripples of conversation go through the people as they look around to find a brave old volunteer. Slowly someone will put a hand up and you can begin to run a little competition to see if there is anyone older than the last person. This doesn't work so well if the oldest person in church is the Vicar; you do need a sprinkling of people in their seventies or eighties present, but that shouldn't be difficult in most Church of England parishes. Once you have determined who the eldest person in church is, find out his or her name (if you don't already know it) and invite that person out to stand with you (offering help if necessary). This can be Simeon or Anna depending on gender, or you can end up with both characters with you. Talk briefly about their role at the Temple in Jerusalem and why they are waiting for the Messiah.

Then – and the people should be ahead of you here – make the same request for the youngest person in church. With any luck this should result in finding a babe in arms. If the parents will allow, and if it is appropriate, bring the child out for all to see and, after introducing the little one to the congregation, present the infant to the oldest person to cuddle. Practical issues need to be considered here: the mum may need to come out with the child and the oldest person may need to be seated, but I've found that even that works because, like the Gospel reading itself, people can see what you're up to because this account is like radio; the mental pictures are better than TV.

The last time I did this, I had found a ninety-three-year-old lady. As soon as it was realized that the job entailed holding a two-week-old baby, another old hand went up for a lady to proclaim that she was ninety-four but had been too bashful to offer herself. Tough. The great-grandmother I had found proudly held the baby, assisted by its parents, while I said that in the recognition of Jesus by Simeon and Anna God recognizes us all who carry the name of his Son, whatever our age or stage in the faith or status in church or society. It is an easy but dramatic way of bringing the generations together. Finally, you might even be able to walk the oldest and youngest around church for all to see before leading the people in reciting the Nunc Dimittis (Luke 2.29–32) together in whatever form is appropriate for the act of worship. Don't get carried away with detail, there is no need to include 'a pair of turtledoves or two young pigeons', but do use this powerful Gospel to value the equal place of all in church, regardless of age or status. It is not difficult to go on from here, perhaps on another occasion, to make the link with the admission of all to Holy Communion.

The only account in the Gospels that refers to Jesus increasing 'in wisdom and in years, and in divine and human favour' is Luke 2.41–52, which is referred to in the next chapter. The twelve-year-old Jesus is shown as being independent of his parents while, in contrast, being dependent on his heavenly Father. This is a confident young Jesus, sure of his valued place in the worshipping community and at home in places of worship. These experiences as a child would have formed the thinking and actions of Jesus when an adult. His clear affection and respect for children are born out of both his own background and his awareness of the importance of childhood to the human condition. So this should be reflected in our response to God's love for his children.

Gospel parallels

The teaching of Jesus in the Gospels is clear, unequivocal and explicit. However, as each evangelist uses the words of Jesus at different times and in differing ways, it can be difficult to pull together a coherent overview to help with promoting the inclusion of children in the central act of the worshipping church. For this reason it's easy for the emphasis of Jesus on the place of children to become diluted, while if read as a whole his teaching in this area is clearer than in many others. One way of looking in overview is to parallel the Synoptic Gospels (Mark, Matthew and Luke) to see how Jesus made abundantly clear his teaching regarding the place of children and how that clarity ought to be represented honestly and openly in the life of the Church.

The dispute about greatness

To be great in God's kingdom, one must be like an innocent child. The three accounts given in Table 2.1 are strikingly similar. Whether in answer to a direct question to him, or by knowing what was stirring among them, or both, Jesus used the same analogy to criticize the disciples' competitive streak and their blindness to the simplicity of faith in God. We can be sure that Jesus is using the example of a child not just as an example of honest commitment but also because there is something in the gift of children that reflects the glory of God. Indeed, in Luke Jesus goes further by identifying the child with Jesus himself and consequently with God himself. The strongest phrase is in Matthew. Jesus says, 'Unless you change and become like children'. Clearly this does not mean we should become childish, but child-like in terms of our relationship with God the Father. For adults this requires a change.

My wife and I have always had a way of dealing with the challenges of ministry, particularly when we are surrounded by people who cannot see the obvious nature of this teaching. We are from ordinary working-class backgrounds and had a modest education. There are always people in church life who know better and don't mind telling you so, particularly if they don't agree with the need to change. They are often highly intelli-

Table 2.1 The dispute about greatness

Mark 9.33–37	Matthew 18.1–5	Luke 9.46–48
Then they came to Capernaum; and when he was in the house he asked them, 'What were you arguing about on the way?' But they were silent, for on the way they had argued with one another who was the greatest. He sat down, called the twelve, and said to them, 'Whoever wants to be first must be last of all and servant of all.' Then he took a little child and put it among them; and taking it in his arms, he said to them, 'Whoever welcomes one such child in my name welcomes me, and whoever welcomes me welcomes not me but the one who sent me.'	At that time the disciples came to Jesus and asked, 'Who is the greatest in the kingdom of heaven?' He called a child, whom he put among them, and said, 'Truly I tell you, unless you change and become like children, you will never enter the kingdom of heaven. Whoever becomes humble like this child is the greatest in the kingdom of heaven. Whoever welcomes one such child in my name welcomes me.'	An argument arose among them as to which of them was the greatest. But Jesus, aware of their inner thoughts, took a little child and put it by his side, and said to them, 'Whoever welcomes this child in my name welcomes me, and whoever welcomes me welcomes the one who sent me; for the least among you is the greatest.'

gent, highly qualified, with good status. However, try to get something practical done or try to speak to hearts and not just minds and then they can't see the wood for the trees. Cathedrals in particular are full of them, but all churches have people whose first approach to their faith is to intellectualize it, often to their own world-view. There is nothing wrong with this; these folk are the raw material of much of church life.

But often the response to God needs to be to open our hearts in faith and not to write a paper on the subject with flow charts

27

or produce a spreadsheet. To 'believe and trust' go together, inseparably, they are two sides of the same commitment. Being on the more intuitive/common-sense side of things, we often find ourselves coming up against such methods when managing change. We have particularly come up against opposition of this nature when promoting the place of children in the Church and within its sacramental life. For example, the disciples, when discussing who was the greatest in the Kingdom of God, were being . . . well, . . . *stupid*. It was obvious that they were getting it wrong but they couldn't see why. So our phrase that keeps us going is that these (good) people are . . . well, . . . *stupid*. Clearly they are not intellectually stupid, but delivery and application are a problem for them. Of course we are all regularly *stupid*, I especially, but Carol and I find the word helps us carry on. It means we have to try harder, be clearer and engage more effectively, perhaps in a language not normally our own. No malice is meant, it just helps us ordinary people cope.

A text which makes this point for me is John 3.1–21. Nicodemus needed to change.

Stumbling blocks

In Mark this verse (see Table 2.2) is part of a group of sayings that act as a warning to would-be disciples, and part of a larger chapter which is concentrating on discipleship and its cost. The chapter begins with the drama of the Transfiguration and includes the discussion about greatness and another foretelling of the Passion. In Chapter 10, Jesus turns towards Jerusalem, so these final sayings from Galilee have real importance. A stumbling block could be people or any policy or practice put in place by people that gets in the way between Jesus and these little ones.

While the chapter is about discipleship, it is clear that Jesus is referring to children here, and very small ones at that. The penalty of getting in the way of such folk who possess this humility is frightening. This millstone is not to be taken lightly. It took a donkey to turn a millstone, it was so large. There is no

Table 2.2 Stumbling blocks

Mark 9.42	Matthew 18.6–7	Luke 17.1–2
'If any of you put a stumbling block before one of these little ones who believe in me, it would be better for you if a great millstone were hung around your neck and you were thrown into the sea.'	'If any of you put a stumbling block before one of these little ones who believe in me, it would be better for you if a great millstone were fastened around your neck and you were drowned in the depth of the sea. Woe to the world because of stumbling blocks! Occasions for stumbling are bound to come, but woe to the one by whom the stumbling block comes!'	Jesus said to his disciples, 'Occasions for stumbling are bound to come, but woe to anyone by whom they come! It would be better for you if a millstone were hung around your neck and you were thrown into the sea than for you to cause one of these little ones to stumble.'

quarter given for getting in the way of these little ones. It's worth thinking about in the context of your own church, your own PCC, and your own worship.

Let the children come to me

How many other people in the Gospels does Jesus so explicitly pray for or over? Taken in date order (see Table 2.3), the Gospels get progressively firmer in describing Jesus' response to the situation. 'Do not stop them' is a command that is, once again, clearer and firmer than many of his other sayings. Many people interpret a degree of anger in his voice in these verses similar to the moment of the cleansing of the Temple. The disciples had spoken sternly and he was not impressed. God's Kingdom is populated by those who, whatever their age – and children exemplify this – can show their dependence on God in simple truth and openness. This is a lesson for the disciples,

Table 2.3 Let the children come to me

Mark 10.13–16	Matthew 19.13–15	Luke 18.15–17
People were bringing little children to him in order that he might touch them; and the disciples spoke sternly to them. But when Jesus saw this, he was indignant and said to them, 'Let the little children come to me; do not stop them; for it is to such as these that the kingdom of God belongs. Truly I tell you, whoever does not receive the kingdom of God as a little child will never enter it.' And he took them up in his arms, laid his hands on them, and blessed them.	Then little children were being brought to him in order that he might lay his hands on them and pray. The disciples spoke sternly to those who brought them; but Jesus said, 'Let the little children come to me, and do not stop them; for it is to such as these that the kingdom of heaven belongs.' And he laid his hands on them and went on his way.	People were bringing even infants to him that he might touch them; and when the disciples saw it, they sternly ordered them not to do it. But Jesus called for them and said, 'Let the little children come to me, and do not stop them; for it is to such as these that the kingdom of God belongs. Truly I tell you, whoever does not receive the kingdom of God as a little child will never enter it.'

and therefore for the whole Church, about teachable humility. It is the children who are the most faithful examples of discipleship in these texts. Luke refers to infants; there is no age limit here. Normally children are expected to become like adults. To enter the Kingdom of God, though, adults must become like children.

Children in the New Testament

The Gospels are explicit about the place of children in the ministry and teaching of Jesus. The rest of the New Testament is more implicit, understanding that children have a rightful place within the Christian community. We are not told exactly what that meant in terms of participation in worship, but children were present and there is no mention of them being excluded at any point. Such a discipline would surely have been mentioned. We can assume therefore that children shared in the Eucharistic worship of the early church on equal terms with adults.

Much of the New Testament concentrates on the nature of relationships within the Christian community. This is especially true in Ephesians (6.1–4) and Colossians (3.20–21). Codes of living for the Christian household are given, including injunctions directly to children themselves. Children are taken seriously by the early church; they are fellow disciples in the Lord, not lesser followers by virtue of their age. They are to be instructed alongside adults. The primary teachers of the faith to them are their parents who are co-workers in the Lord.

This is a mandate for the Church today. The Old Testament tradition has always valued the place of children as a gift from God, the hope of the future. In the New Testament Jesus made plain his love for children and how their openness was a model of discipleship for all those who seek God's Kingdom. Children were full participants in the early church, drawing on the traditions given to them, and the family had a responsibility to teach them the faith as they grew within it to maturity. To withhold baptized children from receiving Christ in the sacrament of the Eucharist is contradictory to the revelation given to us from all of these sources.

3

Millstones and milestones

The process of admission and decision making

Millstones

In Capernaum, on the shores of Galilee, there is a millstone. It is easily missed, being set amidst a display of archaeologically valuable pieces that date from the time of Christ and before. Pilgrims come to see the ruins of the synagogue and the spaceship-like church over the remains of the house of Peter. They don't come to see the millstone, it's just there and there are many others in the Holy Land. But to take this artefact for granted is a mistake.

Remember Matthew 18, a key text in understanding Jesus' emphasis on the place of children. In verse 6, standing in Capernaum, he says:

> If any of you put a stumbling block before one of these little ones who believe in me, it would be better for you if a great millstone were fastened around your neck and you were drowned in the depth of the sea.

Picture the scene. Jesus has already told the disciples that to enter the Kingdom of heaven they must become like children (Matthew 18.1–5). Soon he will rebuke the disciples for getting in the way of the children as they come to Jesus and receive his blessing (Matthew 18.13–15). Here he stands, pointing at a huge millstone, on the shores of a great sea, and to drown with this weight around your neck is a better option than to put something in the way of the little ones who believe in him. The disciples must have been feeling 'got at'. 'Woe to the world because of stumbling blocks' (verse 7).

The church is skilled at turning movements of the Spirit into stumbling blocks. Salt and light become rules and regulations. The challenge for the Church of England in 1997 was to enable the admission of baptized children to Holy Communion in an orderly and sustainable way, which would embody the insights of nurture and all-age belonging, without forcing the issue on one side or alienating families on another side. In short, would structure and legislation be a millstone or a milestone?

Before 1996 only the dioceses of Peterborough, Southwark and Manchester were officially admitting the unconfirmed to Holy Communion, having been given permission on an experimental basis. The pattern was of slow but consistent take-up and participation. Some form of structure for deepening the arrangements was needed if the experiments were to become permanent. Indeed, how could such experiments, once popular, ever retreat? But other factors also came into play. Many clergy were regularly faced at the communion rail with families and children who had been used to receiving elsewhere. This was a particular problem in Local Ecumenical Partnerships, where Free Churches were admitting children to communion as a matter of course. Equally, the practice of admitting to communion before confirmation was growing in other parts of the Anglican Communion and, of course, in many of the European churches.

A survey in 1993 by the National Children's Advisers' Panel, *Unity and Order*, discovered that unconfirmed children were receiving Holy Communion in every diocese, either from their parents or directly from the officiating clergy. This pastoral response to a theological movement was clouded by examples of bad practice that were also discovered. Isolated cases were found but they were serious cases. Born out of a false desire to be nice and without an alternative, it was found that sometimes children were given Smarties or other sweets at the time of communion, or white sliced bread squares. This flawed and counter-productive activity had to be clarified to avoid total confusion. In one famous case, a clergy family was visiting a church one Sunday while on holiday. The children of the family were used to receiving communion and did so reverently. The parents gently warned the children that they might not receive today because the practice of this church might be different. Coming back from the communion rail, the smallest family member proclaimed that he had received communion. All the other children had put their hands out, so he did too. This church, it was found, gave out their Sunday School stamp at the altar rail, and so the child consumed it, being delighted that this church, unlike Daddy's, had communion with pictures on! There are different types of stumbling block.

Enabling change brings milestones of development and progress. Hindering growth and discovery, when inspired by the Spirit, especially when concerning the children Jesus placed so centrally, can be a millstone. The prohibition of administering communion to children has been a millstone around the neck of the Church. We will not know for many years what this heavy weight has done to us. But now, following the process described in Chapter 1, the Church has begun, and only begun, to lift the weight so that we can all walk as equal members of the Body of Christ and be sustained by his sacrificial love. A number of milestones have helped to lift this burden once and for all.

Milestone 1

The House of Bishops' Guidelines
ADMISSION OF BAPTISED PERSONS TO COMMUNION BEFORE CONFIRMATION: Guidelines agreed by the House of Bishops (GS Misc 488)[1]

A. Since 'Communion before Confirmation' is a departure from our inherited norm, it requires special permission. After

34

consultation, every diocesan bishop will have the discretion to make a general policy whether or not to entertain new applications for 'Communion before Confirmation' to take place in his diocese. If he decides to do so, individual parishes must seek his agreement before introducing it. The bishop should satisfy himself that both the incumbent and the Parochial Church Council support any application and that where appropriate, ecumenical partners have been consulted. If the parties cannot agree, the bishop's direction shall be followed.

B. The incumbent must ensure that the policy adopted for his/her parish is clearly and widely understood. The policy should be considered within the general context both of the ministry that is carried out in the parish through initiation, and also of the continuing nurture of people in the Christian faith. The bishop should be satisfied that the programme of continuing Christian nurture is in place leading to confirmation in due course.

C. Before admitting a person to Communion, the priest must seek evidence of baptism. Baptism always precedes admission to Holy Communion.

D. There is a question regarding the age at which children may be admitted to Holy Communion. In general, the time of the first receiving should be determined not so much by the child's chronological age, as by his or her appreciation of the significance of the sacrament. Subject to the bishop's direction, it is appropriate for the decision to be made by the parish priest after consultation with the parents or those who are responsible for the child's formation, with the parents' goodwill. An appropriate and serious pattern of preparation should be followed. The priest and parents share in continuing to educate the child in the significance of Holy Communion so that (s)he gains in understanding with increasing maturity.

E. The Church needs to encourage awareness of many different levels of understanding, and support the inclusion of those with learning difficulties, including children. The incumbent should consult with those concerned in their care, education and support regarding questions of their discernment of the sacrament, their admission to Holy Communion, and their preparation for Confirmation.

F. Before a person is first brought to Holy Communion, the significance of the occasion should be explained to him/her and to his/her parents, and marked in some suitable way before the whole congregation. Whenever possible, the person's family should be involved in the service.

G. A register should be kept of every person admitted to Holy Communion before Confirmation, and each should be given a certificate (or, better, the baptismal certificate should be endorsed).

H. Whether or not a parish practises 'Communion before Confirmation', the incumbent should take care regarding the quality of teaching material, especially that used with children and young people. The material should be reviewed regularly and the advice of diocesan officers and other professional advisers taken into account.

I. The priest must decide exactly how much of the liturgy communicant children will attend. Even if there is a separate 'Ministry of the Word' for children, anyone who is to receive Holy Communion should be present in the main assembly at least for the eucharistic prayer.

J. No baptised person, child or adult, who has once been admitted to Holy Communion and remains in good standing with the Church, should be anywhere deprived of it. When, for example, a family moves to another area, the incumbent of the parish they are leaving should contact their new incumbent to ensure there is no confusion about the communicant status of children. It is the responsibility of the new incumbent to discuss with the children and parents concerned when the children should be presented for Confirmation. Such children should normally be presented by at least the age of 18.

K. Since baptism is at the heart of initiation, it is important for the bishop regularly to be the minister of holy baptism, and particularly at services where candidates will be both baptised and confirmed. It is generally inappropriate for candidates who are preparing for initiation into Christian life in baptism and Confirmation to receive baptism at a service other than the one in which they are to be confirmed.

L. In using rites of public re-affirmation of faith other than baptism and Confirmation, care should be taken to avoid the impression that they are identical with Confirmation. In the case of people who have not been confirmed, it will be more appropriate for the incumbent to propose that they be confirmed.

Milestone 2

Many parishes, about 10 per cent of the church, will be familiar with working out these guidelines. They have served as a useful tool in developing a way forward in this area with its sensitive pastoral, theological and emotional factors. To monitor developments in the dioceses, three questionnaires – **Q1**, **Q2** and **Q3** – were sent out in 2001, 2002 and 2004 respectively. There was a 100 per cent response to all three.

Children and Holy Communion (GS 1576, June 2005) reported the findings of the whole review process. Pages 9–13 show those new to the subject or without easy and regular access to General Synod papers an overview of the national picture.

Q1 asked if the diocese was admitting children, what date implementation had begun, how many churches were admitting children and how many children, approximately or otherwise, were receiving. Those who were not admitting were asked how far the process had gone and what were the future plans, if any. The responses showed that in 2001, the number of dioceses admitting was 37 and the number of churches was 1,064. It became apparent that while there was clarity in the dioceses about the number of churches (not benefices) which had been given permission, not all were recording the number of children. Of the 36 dioceses admitting (excluding London), 15 were keeping no records of numbers of children; 9 estimated 2,510 children and 12 recorded specifically 1,379 children, a total of 3,889 children. Across the five London episcopal areas, two were admitting and keeping no records, two were admitting and recorded 200 children, and one was not admitting at all. This gave an overall total of 4,089.

Q2 omitted the children question altogether and concentrated on church permissions. This was as much to facilitate the process for the dioceses as to elicit as prompt a return as possible. Q2 quite simply reminded each diocese of their Q1 figure and asked them to record any change. Again, there was a 100 per cent response. In 2002, 1,226 churches in 41 out of 47 areas and dioceses had been given permission. This was approximately 8 per cent of the total number of churches nationally.

Q3 was sent out early in 2004 requesting the number of church permissions and numbers of children. The return rate was again 100 per cent and showed that 1,539 churches had been given permission. From those that were recording the numbers, either as an exact number or as a 'guesstimate', 5,515 children were receiving.

It would not be possible to report on the implementation in every diocese in detail. However, to discover how the process was begun, developed and sustained, Manchester, Chichester, Salisbury, Bath and Wells, and Truro have been looked at in some depth.

Of particular interest was how information was produced, how children and congregations were prepared, the impact of the process on clergy, laity, children, congregational life and liturgy, the role of Confirmation and the handling of difference. The Guidelines were not age-specific, but many dioceses settled for somewhere around seven, with Oxford designating a low age of four, and Salisbury choosing not to set an age at all.

The initial tasks for the dioceses included awareness-raising exercises, many producing information/discussion packs for clergy and their congregations. The rationale was that all should debate this issue, that none should feel pressurized, that the traditional pattern of Baptism, Confirmation and Holy Communion was still normative, but that decisions about any future action should be made from an informed, educated basis. Churches which arrived at a 'no, not for us' decision would be encouraged to revisit this issue at some future time, not least because the Guidelines stated quite explicitly that children who had been given permission in one church should not be refused anywhere else.

It has become apparent that most of the perceived problems did not materialize or sorted themselves out, and that where children have been given the opportunity to receive, the whole worshipping life of the congregation has changed and blossomed.

One of the most frequently asked questions has been '. . . but what will happen to Confirmation?' It is early days, but a pattern of better practice seems to be emerging. Some bishops are using the permission-granting process to engage with individual parishes in new and creative ways, especially where commitment to eventual Confirmation is set explicitly at the heart of the permission. The mandate is firmly placed on clergy and congregation to support and sustain contact with the children and their parents.

The evidence of this review of the Guidelines has shown that although the number of churches admitting is proportionately quite small, it is growing steadily. Updates on admission figures offered voluntarily by dioceses, subsequent to the review process, show that the number of churches given permission has increased to 1,650.

A snapshot of the national picture is reproduced here from GS 1576: see Table 3.1 (GS 15761), and the pie charts and graph on page 41 (GS 15762).

Table 3.1 Current diocesan information (GS 15761)

Diocese	Admitting	No. of Churches with Permission
Bath and Wells	Yes	79
Birmingham	Yes	14
Blackburn	Yes	15
Bradford	Yes	131
Bristol	Yes	no figs available yet
Canterbury	Yes	14
Chelmsford	Yes	52
Chester	Yes	42
Chichester	Yes	57
Coventry	Yes	23
Derby	Yes	46
Durham	Yes	54
Ely	Yes	63
Exeter	Yes	3
Gloucester	Yes	53
Guildford	Yes	37
Leicester	Yes	60
Lichfield	Yes	Pilot
Lincoln	Yes	15
Liverpool	Yes	24
London (Edmonton)	Yes	1
London (Kensington Area)	Yes	26
London (Stepney)	Yes	4
London (Two Cities)	Yes	6
London (Willesden Area)	Yes	35
Manchester	Yes	110
Newcastle	Yes	8
Norwich	Yes	100
Oxford	Yes	42
Peterborough	Yes	46
Portsmouth	Yes	7
Ripon and Leeds	Yes	12
Rochester	Yes	32
St Albans	Yes	34
St Edmundsbury and Ipswich	Yes	33
Salisbury	Yes	80
Sheffield	Yes	16
Southwark	Yes	133
Southwell	Yes	54
Truro	Yes	3
Wakefield	Yes	24
Winchester	Yes	27
Worcester	Yes	35
	Total:	1,650
Carlisle	Consultation planned to set policy	
Hereford	Held consultation, no vote yet	
Sodor and Man	No	
York	Under discussion	

GS 15762

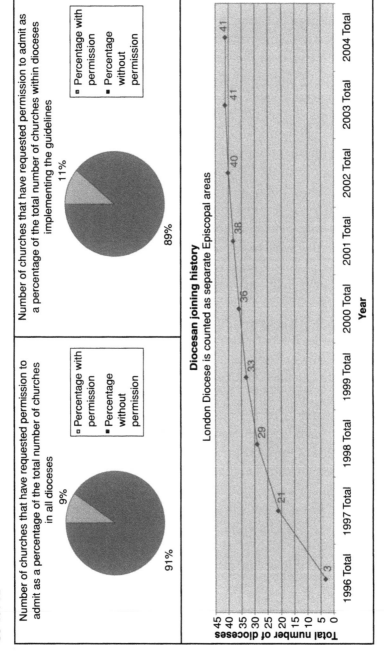

Number of churches that have requested permission to admit as a percentage of the total number of churches in all dioceses

9%

91%

□ Percentage with permission
■ Percentage without permission

Number of churches that have requested permission to admit as a percentage of the total number of churches within dioceses implementing the guidelines

11%

89%

□ Percentage with permission
■ Percentage without permission

Diocesan joining history
London Diocese is counted as separate Episcopal areas

Total number of dioceses

45
40
35
30
25
20
15
10
5
0

3
21
29
33
36
38
40
41
41

1996 Total   1997 Total   1998 Total   1999 Total   2000 Total   2001 Total   2002 Total   2003 Total   2004 Total

Year

Milestone 3

The Bishops' Meeting in June 2004 expressed a desire to firm up the Guidelines into Regulations. Bishop Colin Buchanan recommended strongly that the position should now be normalized through regulations made under Canon B 15A. There was general assent for his proposal.

Canon B 15A (Of admission to Holy Communion) envisages in paragraph 1(c) the admission to Holy Communion of 'any other baptised persons authorized to be admitted under regulations of the General Synod'.

The Board of Education at its meeting in November 2004 agreed to the recommendation that draft regulations should be laid before General Synod for approval, and considered a first draft. At its December 2004 meeting, the House of Bishops Standing Committee gave further consideration to the question whether regulations were necessary. It was suggested that the existing guidelines might suffice. The Church Legal Adviser, Stephen Slack, agreed to prepare advice.

The legal advice was unequivocal. The existing guidelines, issued under paragraph 1(a) of Canon B 15A, 'were, at least in part, intended to facilitate something which paragraph 1(a) of the Canon did not permit – i.e. the admission to Holy Communion of persons not yet "*ready and desirous*" to be confirmed'. Stephen Slack indicated that 'there must be a real risk that, if the guidelines were subjected to legal challenge, the House would be held to have acted unlawfully'.

The advice was that no legal objection could in his view be made to regulations made by the General Synod under paragraph 1(c) of Canon B 15A which allowed the admission to Holy Communion of baptized children who were not yet 'ready and desirous' to be confirmed.

Milestone 4

In July 2005, the Synod was asked to 'take note' of this report (GS 1576) and the accompanying draft regulations.

ADMISSION OF BAPTISED CHILDREN TO COMMUNION DRAFT REGULATIONS 200–

The General Synod hereby makes the following Regulations: –

1. These Regulations may be cited as the Admission of Baptised Children to Communion Regulations 200– and shall come into force on [ ] 200–.
2. Children who have been baptised but who have not yet been confirmed and who are not yet ready or desirous to be confirmed as required by paragraph 1(a) of Canon B 15A may be admitted to Holy Communion provided that the conditions set out in these Regulations are satisfied.
3. Every diocesan bishop may at any time make a direction to the effect that applications from parishes under these Regulations may be made in his diocese. The bishop's discretion in this respect shall be absolute, and he may at any time revoke such a direction (without prejudice to the validity of any permissions already granted thereunder).
4. Where a direction under paragraph 3 is in force in a diocese, an incumbent may apply to the bishop for permission that children falling within the definition in paragraph 2 may be admitted to Holy Communion in one or more of the parishes in the incumbent's charge. Such application must be made in writing and must be accompanied by a copy of a resolution in support of the application passed by the parochial church council of each parish in respect of which the application is made.
5. Before granting any permission under paragraph 4, the bishop must first satisfy himself (a) that the parish concerned has made adequate provision for preparation and continuing nurture in the Christian life and will encourage any child admitted to Holy Communion under these Regulations to be confirmed at the appropriate time and

(b) where the parish concerned is within the area of a local ecumenical project established under Canon B 44, that the other participating Churches have been consulted.

6. The bishop's decision in relation to any application under paragraph 4 shall be final, but a refusal shall not prevent a further application being made on behalf of the parish concerned, provided that at least one year has elapsed since the most recent previous application was refused.

7. Any permission granted under paragraph 4 shall remain in force unless and until revoked by the bishop. The bishop must revoke such permission upon receipt of an application for the purpose made by the incumbent. Such application must be made in writing and accompanied by a copy of a resolution in support of the application passed by the parochial church council of each parish in respect of which the application is made.

8. Where a permission granted under paragraph 4 is in force, the incumbent shall not admit any child to Holy Communion unless he or she is satisfied that (a) the child has been baptised and (b) the persons having parental responsibility for the child are content that the child should be so admitted. Otherwise, subject to any direction of the bishop, it is within the incumbent's absolute discretion to decide whether, and if so when, any child should be admitted to Holy Communion.

9. The incumbent shall maintain a register of all children admitted to Holy Communion under these Regulations, and where practicable will record on the child's baptismal certificate the date and place of the child's admission. If the baptismal certificate is not available, the incumbent shall present the child with a separate certificate recording the same details.

10. A child who presents evidence in the form stipulated in paragraph 9 that he or she has been admitted to Holy Communion under these Regulations shall be so admitted at any service of Holy Communion conducted according to the rites of the Church of England in any place, regardless

of whether or not any permission under paragraph 4 is in force in that place or was in force in that place until revoked.

11. These Regulations shall apply to a cathedral as if it were a parish, with the modifications that:

   (a) any application under paragraphs 3 or 7 must be made by the dean of the cathedral concerned, accompanied by a copy of a resolution in support of the application passed by the chapter of the cathedral concerned;

   (b) the obligations imposed on the incumbent under paragraphs 8 and 9 shall be imposed on the dean of the cathedral concerned.

12. A diocesan bishop may delegate any of his functions under these Regulations (except his functions under paragraph 3) to a person appointed by him for the purpose, being a suffragan or assistant bishop or archdeacon of the diocese.

13. In these Regulations:

   (a) 'incumbent', in relation to a parish, includes:

      (i) in a case where the benefice concerned is vacant (and paragraph (ii) below does not apply), the rural dean;

      (ii) in a case where a suspension period (within the meaning of the Pastoral Measure 1983) applies to the benefice concerned, the priest-in-charge; and

      (iii) in a case where a special cure of souls in respect of the parish has been assigned to a vicar in a team ministry by a Scheme under the Pastoral Measure 1983 or by licence from the bishop, that vicar; and

   (b) references to paragraph numbers are to be to the relevant paragraph or paragraphs in these Regulations.

The Board of Education at its meeting in May 2005 considered the draft regulations, prepared by the legal Office on the basis of the Board's discussion, and agreed that they should be laid before the General Synod for general discussion.

Milestone 4

The debate in General Synod in July 2005 was significant in that as well as responding for the request for a review, as agreed in 2000, a legal loophole had been found, requiring a firmer foundation for any such guidelines. The review process showed steady growth in the number of parishes seeking permission to admit children to communion before confirmation. Figures showed that the number of churches admitting children to communion was growing year by year – up from 1,064 in 2001 to 1,650 by the middle of 2005. This meant that children were being admitted in about 10 per cent of parishes. While in some places the actual number of children being admitted was small, participating churches of all types reported that the process of debate and implementing the guidelines had re-energized their worship and nurture programmes.

During the debate theological and other issues were batted to and fro but in an atmosphere of general understanding and acceptance by the members of the Synod that this was a subject whose day had come. It was said that children admitted to communion took it very seriously; that there was a lower drop-out rate than with the traditional pattern of teenage confirmation; that children were the best apostles to other children, who 'clamoured' to join them at the altar. Some concerns, more about good practice than principle, were raised, such as unconfirmed adults coming new to the Church who were unable to receive communion, but parish clergy seemed used to dealing with such pastoral moments as opportunities more than problems.

A telling contribution came from the Very Revd Archimandrite Ephrem Lash, the representative on the General Synod of the Orthodox Churches. He stated that as many as had been baptized had put on Christ. 'If you have put on Christ, you are a full Christian.' He could not understand how someone born again of water and the Holy Spirit could then be starved for fourteen years. It was proper for the Church to have a rite of passage for teenagers: 'I don't want to deprive bishops of their moment of glory,' he said. For Ephrem, the idea of confirmation as a reaffirming of baptismal vows did not make sense. 'Christian initiation is a once-for-all introduction into life, into which you grow.' He concluded by reminding the Synod that many of the Fathers were not baptized until around the age of thirty, and concluded: 'If you are going to be baptized, you should be admitted to communion straight away.' At the end of the debate members overwhelmingly took note of the report, knowing that the General Synod in November 2005 would be asked to give draft approval.

So in November the new membership of the General Synod met for the first time, with five years of work in front of them. These first two days included much work carried over from the last Synod, including the draft Regulations described above. But the day, hopefully like subsequent meetings of Synod, was characterized by a strong lead from the Archbishop of Canterbury describing his hopes for how a synod should reflect a way of working for the whole Church. He said, in part of his Presidential Address:

> That is why you are here. You are here to take responsibility for a vision. You have been elected perhaps to serve a particular kind of vision within the spectrum of our Church. Once you are here, however, you are also committed, just by being here and praying together, to listen and look for a vision which is that of the whole Church, a vision which is in accord with God's purpose for his people. Synod is, in the full, ancient sense of the word, a Catholic body or it is nothing. It is an organ of the Church's constant search for a fuller grasp of the all-encompassing mystery in the middle of which it lives and prays.

The debate in Synod regarding Admission was to be solely on the regulations themselves, which would be sent on to the House of Bishops before coming back to the Synod at the earliest opportunity. It was a short debate, opened again by the Bishop of Dover. His opening statement made the continuation of this work from the last synod and previous synods clear. This statement was an important milestone as many on synod were coming to this subject for the first time, and, while we were confident that this legislation would move forward, this was the first time that the mind of the new synod would be tested. This statement is also a useful summary of all that had gone before. Bishop Venner said:

> I hope that members who have been on Synod before will forgive me, but I need to start with two bits of information for those who are new. The first is an example of the care with which those who determine and facilitate our business use language, together with one of our arcane but important processes.
>
> We are today discussing Admission of Baptized Children to Holy Communion Regulations. In other words, we are not today discussing the issue of whether or not baptized children should be welcomed to the Lord's Table; that is already happening, thank God. No. I am asking Synod to consider a particular set of regulations which will go to the House of Bishops for formal approval in January, and hopefully return for final approval by Synod next February.
>
> Secondly, I need to beg the indulgence of experienced members of Synod and briefly tell the story of how we have got to where we are. That story is explained in the blue background paper, GS 1596X. Since the 1950s – which some of us will remember – and the growth of the Parish Communion, there has been a growing theological awareness of baptism as the one complete rite of initiation. Baptized children are wholly, and not conditionally, in the Body of Christ. As such, they are part of the sacramental community and should, with appropriate nurturing and support, be welcomed at the communion rail with adults.
>
> The debate has continued more formally for nearly 40 years, beginning with the National Evangelical Congress at Keele in 1967. Over the following 20 years a momentum built up. A number of provinces of the Communion admitted children to the

sacrament. Children began to feature more and more on the mission agenda of dioceses and parishes, helped by a number of reports, including most particularly in this regard *Children in the Way*, published in 1988, and *ON the WAY* in 1995.

In November 1996, the General Synod agreed the House of Bishops' Guidelines on the Admission of Baptized Persons to Holy Communion before Confirmation. This permitted and encouraged churches to explore the nature of the sacrament and the question of who should receive, including children. It was built on the foundation of Canon B 15A(a) – which members will immediately recall! Just in case it has slipped your memory, it permits the admission to Holy Communion of 'members of the Church of England who . . . are ready and desirous of being confirmed'.

Since then, the practice has grown gently but surely, more by evolution than by revolution, as parishes have considered the question and felt the need. Last July I reported that some 10 per cent of parishes across the Church of England are now admitting children to communion in 37 out of the 43 English dioceses. However, along with that, less happily, a survey of diocesan children's advisers in 1993 revealed that there were numerous examples of uncanonical and, I have to say, un-desirable practices. I am not going to tell you about them, as they might give you ideas! It is rather like those old preparation booklets which we used to get before confirmation, which gave you a list of sins that you might like to confess. I got some very good ideas from that!

Clergy found themselves in difficult pastoral situations. With people becoming increasingly mobile, the arrival in their congregations of families whose children had been receiving communion elsewhere was becoming more frequent and raising challenges, as some children did receive while others from Christian families did not.

As we have considered all of this we have also realized that the original decision to base our practice upon the phrase 'ready and desirous of being confirmed' was disingenuous, as indeed we had been told by Bishop Colin Buchanan and many others. So the Board of Education returned to a recommendation of the Knaresborough Report in 1985, that we should instead look to Canon B 15A(c), with which I am sure you would all readily concur. Again, just in case it has slipped your mind, Canon B 15A(c) says, 'any other baptized persons, authorized to be admitted under regulations of the General Synod'. It is those regulations that are before you today. If Synod gives them a fair wind this morning, they will be referred to the House of Bishops under Article 7 of the General Synod Constitution, since they touch on the administration of the Sacraments, before they come back in February for final approval.

It is important for us to remember that, for most churches, the traditional process of baptism, confirmation, then first communion is still normal practice. However, these regulations allow bishops to permit parishes to admit children before confirmation, if his conditions and criteria are met. It is a practice that Synod warmly acknowledged last July, as we heard some very moving stories of the impact that children receiving alongside us adults has had, not just on them but upon us and upon other people. The decision therefore is not whether children should receive but how each parish and diocese should enable it to happen.

These regulations build on experience of good practice and, as you would expect, set out clearly the processes involved. Much more importantly, they encourage parishes to explore together the nature of the sacrament and the question of who should receive. This discussion is an opportunity not just to talk about children but to explore how all the people of God can be helped to appreciate and value this gift of God more profoundly. Children will not only be prepared for receiving Holy Communion, but there will also be, and should be, a process of continuing nurture in the Christian life, leading them to confirmation in due course.

As Bishop David Stancliffe has written elsewhere,

> It is our Anglican custom to offer 'eucharistic hospitality' to all who come to the altar. . . . We don't ask probing questions or demand pledges to the club rules. All we ask

is that those who come should have been baptized in the name of the Holy Trinity. Our custom is born . . . of a deep theological conviction that the altar table is the Lord's and that it is not for us to place boundaries around it. . . . The invitation is Christ's, and those who respond to it are drawn into communion not just with their neighbours . . . but with the one who has called them and feeds them with the Body and Blood of his Son.

So enabling our children to respond to Christ's invitation with us becomes not just our gift to them, but their gift to us. I therefore ask Synod to consider these regulations, and to do so positively.

So once again, the vast majority of speakers welcomed the Regulations as a necessary statement required on the way to full permission. A few speakers lapsed back into commenting on the principle of admitting children, and that was inevitable with a new membership, but it was noticeable that some seemed to want regulation of almost every issue, not just this one. There was a request for more statistical information to back up the need for such regulations and for less emphasis on anecdotal stories, but it was clear that this is essentially a pastoral issue and not easily measurable. The time for a review would be after full permission had been given, and then after a period of years for a true picture of take-up and practice, in order to give a sensible overview. A useful contribution was made about those with 'parental care for children' and this would be reflected in the final regulations. Some sought reflection not just on inviting people to communion based on their baptismal status but on their 'good standing' – a phrase often used by the Church. The problem, it seemed to me, is that there is always a fine line between good order and asking more, in particular of children, than we do of adults. How do we determine 'good standing' among adults who present themselves for Holy Communion? We cannot ask more of our children than we do of our adults. Many speakers testified to good experiences, having become converts to this engagement with children, and in the end the vote was decisively won. The Regulations therefore went to the House of Bishops for final approval before coming back to Synod in February 2006, for one more milestone.

Milestone 5

The Archbishops' Council was set up in 1999 to 'co-ordinate, promote, aid and further the work and mission of the Church of England'. Archbishop George Carey spoke of the Council having a vision for the Church which should be outward-looking, united and confident. The following statement of purpose has been made by the Archbishops' Council:

> Working as one body, to serve the Church of England through the power of the Holy Spirit, by supporting, promoting and extending the mission, ministry and witness of the Church to the nation.

The Council has a wide-ranging brief which includes 'the encouragement of the Church's ministry among children and young people and enabling lifelong learning within the Church'. In 2001, the Archbishops' Council published a report (GS Misc 650) setting out four themes for its future work. Underpinning the four themes are two fundamentals for the Church, which the Council holds to be integral to the very being of the Church and which will be reflected both in their own right and in the way in which work under the themes is pursued. These are worship and the quest for full visible unity.

The four themes which the Council set itself to pursue as a particular focus for its work over the period 2000–5 were:

- engaging with social issues;
- equipping to evangelize;
- welcoming and encouraging children and young people;
- developing the ministry of all.

Unpacking these priorities the Council stated this definition:

> Welcoming and encouraging children and young people – To welcome and encourage children and young people, and to be encouraged by them, and to engage with them on their spiritual journey wherever they are.

Clearly, in the highest councils of the Church, a commitment to the place of children in the Church had been articulated. While this means a range of subject areas will always be important in working with children, it would be impossible for the Church to retreat in the welcoming of children in worship and in particular their sharing with adults in the Eucharistic meal. This has been enshrined in an important milestone for the Church: *Sharing the Good News with Children: The Church of England's Strategy for Children*. Passed by the General Synod in July 2003 this is a joint strategy from the former Boards of Mission and Education, now the Mission and Public Affairs and the Education divisions. The National Children's Officer, Diana Murrie, and the Archbishop's Officer for Evangelism among Children, Margaret Withers, worked closely together on the implementation of the strategy but each had areas of particular responsibility.

Responses by churches have been piecemeal. The strategy draws them together by affirming present good practice and giving a basis for dioceses and parishes to develop their ministry among children in parishes, schools and the wider community. Has your parish studied this strategy? If not, ask yourself what this says about the importance of children in your congregation. The Key Areas of the Strategy can be viewed at <www.cofe.anglican.org/faith/mission/strategy>.

Key Area 1 states the following aims:

1. Children, worship and nurture

To enable children to develop spiritually and to come to form a relationship with God through his Word, sacraments, personal prayer and contact with other Christians that is appropriate to their age, culture and stage of faith

1. To explore the ways in which children are involved in the worship of the Church, including Eucharistic worship, and identify and disseminate examples of good practice and creative use of liturgies with children present
2. To come to a common mind about the knowledge that we expect children to have of the Christian faith as discovered through Scripture, being part of the Church, and Christian living, according to their ages, cultures and abilities
3. To equip children to make moral and social decisions and develop lively and searching attitudes to values and attitudes in society as well as in their faith.

So if the primary aim of the Church's ministry among children is their spiritual development, it is impossible to segregate them from the primary sacramental source of spiritual development for Christians. It is easy to sound polemical but if the Church has at last been able to encapsulate its thinking about work with children, it is not surprising that conclusions can be drawn, and changes to the life of the Church found to be necessary. Some might say this is a very 'C of E' way of doing things, through committees, structures and statements, but, as is so often the case in Anglican liturgy, what we say together describes what we believe together and now, at last, the place of children in the worship of the Church has been recognized. If this is the case, the next step is for the Church to come to a common mind about the aims of a nurture programme or to use the old word, a catechism, so that children may be prepared with confidence for their on-going growth as Christians in the world. Enquiring minds and spiritual openness are gifts that children bring to the Church but these gifts do not last long as life goes on. Children's attitudes are largely formed by the time they are eight so the Church's key work must start with the very young. Their early, positive experiences of worship and good Christian nurture will help them to continue to develop spiritually as they move towards and through their experiences as a teenager.

Another milestone

As I'm sitting here writing all of this stuff, children from one of our local church schools are standing outside my study window. I wish this book was more interactive and that you could hear their informal singing. They've just been in the cathedral, preparing for their Eucharist later today. Obviously enthused by what they have been doing, and for what is to come, they are singing, beautifully and proudly, on the pavement as the world goes by, the hymn 'My Jesus, my Saviour'. They are not self-conscious, they are not embarrassed, they are not adults; they are Christians, they are Anglicans. Enough said!

> My Jesus, my Saviour
> Lord there is none like You
> All of my days, I want to praise
> The wonders of Your mighty love
>
> My comfort, my shelter
> Tower of refuge and strength
> Let every breath, all that I am
> Never cease to worship You
>
> Shout to the Lord
> All the earth let us sing
> Power and majesty
> Praise to the King
> Mountains bow down
> And the seas will roar
> At the sound of Your name
>
> I sing for joy
> At the work of Your hands
> Forever I'll love You
> Forever I'll stand

Nothing compares to the promise
I have in You

Milestones elsewhere

The Church of England has finally come to an awareness of the importance of admitting children to Holy Communion. In other churches, this has also either been a process of discernment or a long-established practice.

Orthodox Church: The link between baptism and communion for infants is considered to be part of the apostolic tradition and therefore as normal as it is important. Baptism, followed by Chrismation and communion, are part of the one act of initiation. Infants receive communion, often on a spoon, and are part of the community of faith in Christ.

Roman Catholic Church: While baptism is administered to infants, the link with receiving communion is combined with prior instruction and first confession. As a general rule, children are admitted to first communion, often in special services, around the age of seven. The Roman Catholic Church has made significant efforts to develop its liturgy for the active participation of children, including the provision of particular Eucharistic prayers.

Methodist Church: In 1987 the Methodist Conference in England approved the report *Children at Holy Communion: Guidelines* which found no inconsistency between admitting children to communion and Wesley's own practice and teaching. Wesley regularly gave communion to children at his own services. The rather sensible and pragmatic approach of Methodists is that the gospel should be told to young enquirers in ways appropriate to them and then they should be invited to share in the Lord's Supper if they desire it.

Baptist Churches: The Baptists maintain the honourable conviction that communion is linked to baptism which follows a mature declaration of faith and commitment.

Anglican Communion: Across the provinces of the Anglican Communion the position is varied. Children receive communion in Canada, Australia, New Zealand and South Africa and the United States of America. In many places, the practice depends on the permission of the local archbishop or diocesan bishop.

One last milestone

For enthusiasts, or for those who have discovered the positive changes that this long process has brought to parish life, even the milestones of change will have been too far apart. But in the scheme of things that is life in the Church a careful, sensitive process of change is longer lasting and more inclusive. In February 2006, the General Synod was to discuss the final regulations for final approval. This debate is discussed in the concluding chapter. Would the Church finally let the children come and with what degree of enthusiasm?

Notes

1 Reports and Proceedings of the General Synod can be viewed online at <www.cofe.anglican.org/about/gensynod/>.

For a full and frank description of the synodical process, read Colin Buchanan, *Taking the Long View: Three and a half decades of General Synod* (Church House Publishing, 2006), chap. 5: 'Children in communion'.

4

Personally speaking

Interviews with church leaders

Have you ever been lost as a child? If you have, you'll know it's a horrible feeling. Yesterday I went to Marks & Spencer (as you do) and clearly a child had been lost and, despite the discreet and efficient assistance of the staff, the frightened mother was calling the child's name at the top of her voice. Shouting out like that in a shop is something which breaks the order of things and is disconcerting. It was the mother's calling which found the child. I was once lost on a summer's day, on a huge Dorset beach, for about four hours. I suppose I was seven or eight years old. As time wore on I became scared, very scared. Eventually I wandered back in the right direction and my frantic parents were cross and delighted in their relief in equal amounts. It's the sort of thing that happens every day but I remember it as one of the most vivid moments of my childhood.

Today many parents are unwilling to let their children out of their sight. We have changed as a community. I used to play out on the road as a kid, my children never have. Times have changed. In the time of Jesus it was normal for the wider family, the community of faith, to share in caring for children. In Luke 2.41–52 we see Jesus travelling to Jerusalem with his parents for the festival of the Passover. When it is time to return, Mary and Joseph are so trusting of their fellow travellers that they assume Jesus is in the group – somewhere. They travel for a whole day before checking on his whereabouts. As parents we would never have done that, it would simply never happen, we would have to know where our three were at all times. Most people would be the same. Either the Holy Family were a bit dysfunctional or it was normal for this sort of confidence to be placed in the wider circle of family and friends. And this went on for a whole day, not a minute or two in M&S or four hours on a beach, but a 'day's journey'. The Gospel says that Mary and Joseph simply assumed Jesus was there; this sort of thing was OK for a twelve-year-old. They searched for Jesus but didn't find him for three days!

At last, no doubt at their wits' end, they finally check the Temple and there he is 'sitting among the teachers, listening to them and asking them questions'. Mary and Joseph were 'astonished', which puts it mildly, I expect. Jesus' reply to his mother's question would have earned a clip round the ear in my day but of course this unique account of Jesus' maturing is there to make a point. Where else could Jesus have been but in his Father's house, sitting among the teachers who were amazed at his understanding and answers? A visit to the Western (Wailing) Wall puts all this in perspective as visitors are welcome to watch Jewish boys of this same sort of age expounding the scriptures at their bar mitzvah. It is a moving and holy sight to behold, a community event. Mary and Joseph did not fully understand the meaning of all this but were no doubt mightily relieved when Jesus returned with them, was obedient and, as he grew, increased in wisdom and in 'divine and human favour'.

Having a child sit with the teachers of the day was the inspiration of this chapter. There are issues with 'letting the children come . . .' to communion that are best dealt with by sitting down with the teachers of the day and hearing what they have to say. I have conducted a number of interviews, some with a very nice lunch, to widen the scope of this subject as far as possible and to hear what practitioners and church leaders themselves have to say about the admission of children to communion before confirmation. The interviews were deliberately informal and conversational in style. I am grateful to those interviewed for being open and confident enough to be able to speak from the heart.

The task is to see how the Church is moving together as a pilgrim community, and, this time, with the children with us rather than left behind.

Interview 1
Baptism and admission to Holy Communion
David Stancliffe
Bishop of Salisbury

I wanted to talk to the Bishop of Salisbury about baptism, confirmation, bishops and the place of children. In particular, why is an understanding of the importance of Holy Baptism so important for an understanding of the need to welcome children to communion? Bishop David is a scholar and pastor with a confidence born of hard work and a commitment to the people of his diocese. My eldest child well remembers him popping into the Vicarage one evening while on the way to a service. Not everyone can say that a Diocesan Bishop has helped tuck them into bed for the night. She can still impersonate his voice rather well.

Bishop Stancliffe recently stepped down after twelve years as Chairman of the Church of England's Liturgical Commission. Before that he was a curate in Leeds, a school chaplain in Bristol, a cathedral precentor and a Director of Ordinands before being Provost of Portsmouth, where with a talented team of colleagues – three others of whom are now bishops – he completed and re-ordered the unfinished cathedral as a focus for the life of the parish, city and diocese. He is passionate about the Sudan – Salisbury's twinned province – and about early music, and has written about his enthusiasms in his book *God's Pattern*.

'Bishop David, how important is it to you, as a bishop, to baptize?'

'Let's start back a step. When I was putting a new font into the cathedral at Portsmouth, I had in mind that there were people coming to the cathedral from all over the diocese who were new to the faith but had been nurtured and brought by their parish priests to one of the frequent Saturday evening celebrations of baptism and confirmation we did there. But there were also, as we were also an actual parish and people lived in all the houses around, members of the regular congregation and parishioners who brought their children for baptism. There I was looking to create a font in which I could baptize people of any age properly. And I think it's my experience of being able to put people under the water and holding their hand as they lost their sense of balance as they went through the waters and stepped out the other side that was a powerful and formative one in my experience of baptizing.

'Then having come to Salisbury where I am without a church of my own in that sense, I'm delighted to find the Dean and Chapter at the stage where they are currently looking for a new and invigorating font for the nave of the cathedral and getting the celebration of baptism out of the little Victorian side chapel where it's hidden. This chimes in exactly with what I want to say about baptism being the foundation of our life in Christ, the foundation of our call as Christian disciples from which springs any call to use our particular gifts and exercise particular ministries. I regard a visible sign of baptism as hugely important, especially if you go to celebrate a confirmation in a parish church where there happen to be no candidates for baptism. If everyone there's already been baptized, it's difficult to convince the candidates for confirmation that they are recapping on this great dying to self and rising to new life in Christ when the font looks like a birdbath and a sign of Christ's death and resurrection simply isn't visible.

'When I first came to Salisbury I found that in many cases parish priests assumed that if a confirmation candidate had not been baptized this was an unfortunate omission and they ought to be baptized secretly in private before I got there. I had to stop all that straight away and say, "No, the most important thing in relation to people coming into and growing into the faith and starting their journey of discipleship is that I'm there with them at the moment of their baptism. That's far more important than their confirmation." What I found was that, as in most of the rest of the Church, many people in Salisbury hadn't really thought of baptism as anything else than an infant rite, and they hadn't seen the intimate connection between baptism and confirmation or the importance of the bishop as the president at baptism.

'I mean, I don't mind too much about presiding at confirmation; I would gladly delegate to the presbyters of the diocese those "cauldrons of consecrated oil" as Bishop Hensley Henson once rather wryly called the anointing at confirmation. But I do mind very much about being there at and presiding over the moment when new Christians come to make their affirmation of faith for the first time. I'm very happy to delegate parts of the rite like the signing with the cross and the water baptism to my fellow presbyters, but being there to preside over those rites is a matter of importance to me as the one charged with the apostolic leadership and mission of the diocese. If the diocese isn't known to be making disciples and the bishop isn't seen to be actively engaged not only in telling people to do it but actually doing it himself, then I think something crucial is missing.'

'Bishop, if that is the case, what is the place of Confirmation? Some are concerned about what happens to this treasured moment if it's not linked to communion.'

'For adults the key moment is often very clear. If they've not been baptized, they come to faith and pursue the pattern in a logical order. As they come up out of the waters and you anoint them, praying over them that they may grow in the life of the Spirit there and then, the question in my mind is, why it is necessary to go on to confirm them? At the moment, of course, something separate called "Confirmation" is part of what the Canons – Church law – require, but adult baptism by the bishop combined with Chrismation and a generous prayer for living in the life of the Holy Spirit seems to me to be perfectly enough. I think that's true of Christians who ask for baptism at any age and that's why I have no problem with baptizing and Chrismating and then communicating the newly baptized, because I believe that all the baptized belong together inescapably – children and adults together of any age who are presented to me. I remember once going on a Sunday to an ordinary Parish Communion in one of the parishes in the diocese, and the parish priest said to me that this was the first Sunday they were admitting children to communion: going along rows and rows and rows of children of all ages, from infants in arms through to six- and seven-year-olds from the local school, to those adults who had recently come to faith themselves, was an experience which I remember vividly to this day. That's how it ought to be. I mean either you are baptized and so are *in Christo* or you are not; and once you are, you cannot exclude those baptized into Christ from the fullness of living in Christ, which means belonging in his Body, the Church, and receiving the sacrament of his body and blood in the Eucharist. You can of course only be initiated into the life of Christ once, but once you're baptized you're baptized!

'I'm all for helping the baptized, whatever age they come and whoever they're brought by, to receive the sacrament. Sometimes it's parents or grandparents that bring them; but sometimes it's school-mates who bring them to the school Eucharist. Small children can be wonderful apostles in that sense and often bring their parents into faith too.

'I remember in the parish where I was trained as a curate it was adults bringing their children to baptism that was the most significant moment of challenge in our discipling activity. Those new parents were at the point where they were being faced with the responsibility of bringing a child into the world and having to care for it and nurture it, and this automatically raised a question for themselves: they had to say "How does this faith thing relate to me?" Our confirmation classes even in the late sixties were substantially adult with some teenagers rather than the other way round, and at that stage the trigger for their own commitment was very often bringing their children to baptism.

'We need to see these stages in the life of the Church as all belonging together. There's not one called "the baptism of infants" and another thing called "the baptism of adults", nor even something called "baptism followed some time later by a mysterious thing called confirmation which admits you to communion". We now understand that it's baptism that is our full and once-and-for-all initiation into Christ from which everything else follows. That's why I'm very pleased liturgically that we've made more of baptism, and restored anointing with Chrism to the baptism service; that prayer 'May God, who has received you by baptism into his Church, pour upon you the riches of his grace', which accompanies sealing with Chrism, is the only prayer that I've ever written that nobody's ever mucked around with: it sailed straight through the lengthy processes of revision and authorization. I did say to the House of Bishops, when I introduced them to it, that this is the essential heart of the fullness of baptism which some people have described as confirmation.

'It's the emphasis on the work of the Spirit and not just the water baptism, the initiation of the new creation and the beginning of life growing into the fullness of life in Christ, and being the recipient of the gifts of the Spirit, that complements going under the waters, the dying and rising in Christ that Easter offers. Uniting these two strands is an enormously important thing that we've done in the revised baptism rite. I did say to the bishops, "You know, this is essentially a confirmation prayer." But although there was some understandable nervousness about whether the bishops would lose their *raison d'être*, because they mightn't find they were going round confirming all the time, I also said to them, "Don't worry; there may be less people coming forward to confirm but in a missionary world there will be a great deal more coming forward to be baptized and that's where you should be directing the spearhead of your ministry."

'But of course confirmation does present its opportunities too: it is important for people to have the opportunity to affirm their faith publicly, and to do that before the bishop as a representative of the universal Church. Confirmation brings us together. And confirmation has its own power: people often come to you afterwards and say things like "This reminds me of my own confirmation, but it wasn't anything like this in those days; how I wish I could be confirmed again: I'd love to be able to recommit myself in the life I'm trying to live today." And why not? Why can people not come to more mature understandings of their faith in changing circumstances, whether triggered by big events such as starting a family or changing job or disasters such as the death of a partner? Whatever it is, people do come to significant moments of faith in a variety of ways and I'm one of those who think that the possibility of re-affirming your faith in a bold way, with the use of all the signs that we use in confirmation, anointing and the laying on of hands and prayer for the filling of the person with the power of the Holy Spirit, is something that we should be doing more and more regularly and not treat as the once in a lifetime event that the initial baptism is and must be. So although we have put into *Common Worship* services for the Affirmation of Baptismal Faith with a different prayer over a candidate, but still with the laying on of hands, I really think that's unnecessary and that we should be using the same rite as for anybody who is being confirmed.'

'Bishop, what you're describing demands a real engagement, both liturgically and in mission terms, between the presiding minister and the candidates. How would you link what we do in church with what it means to people's lives of faith?'

'This takes us back into questions about baptism. If a baptism is celebrated well with understanding by the host community and is clearly a delight rather than a bore to the person who is presiding, it can be a life-changing experience for a family. When a family bring a child to church in order to "get it done" and actually then find they're taken seriously (and their own level of faith and understanding is taken seriously too), then the doors begin to open. I well remember once visiting your last parish, Stephen, for a confirmation service, and in order to ensure there was at least one baptism, you persuaded a young family, who were on the very fringe of the church, to have their baby's baptism in that same service.

'It was very brave of them, so I wanted to make a fuss of them and not lose the importance of what we'd done for the child after all that confirming of the confirmation candidates later in the service. So in the final hymn I retrieved the infant and carried it around the church for all to see. It made the point so well that what we were celebrating was God's love, his gift, not our faith. Now I've learnt that since then the mother of the child has been confirmed as have the child's grandparents, and one of them is now Churchwarden!

'It does work, and people's lives can be changed by liturgy being brought to life from mere words on paper to a dynamic expression of what God is doing for his people in Christ. Reflecting on what can happen, all unknowingly, just encourages me to go on spending time in parishes doing things other than celebrating the Eucharist. It's often assumed, you know, that what you are there to do on a Sunday, quite properly too, is to preside at the Eucharist for the church – to celebrate that sacrament of belonging in Christ, forging community, helping a scattered group of people grow up into something beyond themselves, bigger than themselves, as they grow up into the Body of Christ and become part of the Church universal. That's fine, but it might also be quite appropriate to go to a church as the bishop primarily for a baptism, and if you celebrate that baptism fully and richly that may be more than enough for one service. That's one of the things I want to encourage my fellow bishops to be doing – that a Sunday morning spent primarily baptizing, primarily engaging with new disciples, will be time well spent.

'There are ways too, even if they are very slender, of keeping in touch with and encouraging those new disciples. I often ask people to send me a postcard on the first anniversary of their baptism and confirmation, telling me what difference it's made to their lives and just one of the things they've started doing as a result. A large number of those cards come in and they're very special.

'I also think it's important that bishops play a part in challenging the baptized to live out the baptized life. We spend a lot of time beforehand preparing candidates, but in the early days of the Church the bishop used to sit down with them after baptizing them to ask what this had meant for them and how they were going to work it out with a Rule of Life; "How are you going to fit in working at the soup kitchen and when is your study time?", things like that. There doesn't seem to be much time for this these days, and that's where the partnership between bishop and parish priests is so important. But people are often surprised and delighted to sit down with their bishop, talking to them about such things rather than internal church matters like pastoral reorganization or such mindnumbing topics. One of the things I ask of young people is to ring me on the night before they're eighteen to tell me three good reasons, if they can find them, why they shouldn't be ordained.

'I'm keen to challenge their sense of vocation; it may sound like a sound-bite but they do occasionally ring and more often write with the wriggling excuses, which reveal a lively faith. At the very least we ought to be challenging people with the expectation that if they're baptized and confirmed, and they've tumbled to it that that's who they are, then God will have given them gifts, and it's up to them to use them in his service. It's our shared task to help them discover how to best do that: this is an equally important part of the Church's mission. So often we're great at getting people in and celebrating such moments as their confirmation; but then we abandon them because we're on to the next lot. Who are we training to take on the development of people seriously? That's why, of course, in our admitting baptized children to communion we've set up such a good pattern, because, yes, we've done some minimal preparation of children about the rite and they're excited to be included and to receive and they can learn from some of the excellent courses about how to get started. But more importantly, and this is reflected in the only absolute condition I lay down – it's nothing about age or anything ridiculous like that – I insist that there is adequate nurture and follow-up to help people grow. And how do you expect people to grow if we're not regularly feeding them with both the sacrament and teaching? – and this is equally important for adults as it is for children.'

'Bishop, you have been involved in the evolution of children receiving communion from the beginning of the process in the Church of England. How would you describe what has gone on in terms of growing awareness and understanding?'

'As background to the Church's thinking about admitting children to Holy Communion, a small group was appointed to produce the strategy paper ON the WAY. This group was set up with two people each from the Board of Education, the Board of Mission and the Liturgical Commission. It was a very small group but all were engaged in the continuing question of how to link mission and worship with belief and belonging. We sat down to what we thought was going to be a very long meeting, coming from different traditions and different starting points, but discovered within an hour that we had a common mind on most of the key issues.

'Whether we were starting from the liturgical tradition or from the educational models, or primarily from the desire to create a realistic engagement with mission, we had the same values, and after a single half day's meeting we had a framework we could build upon. That is an important bit of background. From that agreement, the work we put through Synod on admitting children to communion had that kind of feel to it. I had to talk the Synod through the theological issues and the sense of consensus we'd had in the group about it came through. I know I was very clear that the theological thrust was admitting people to communion on the basis of their baptism rather than admitting people to communion before confirmation. It's not a question of doing something before confirmation, it's a question of doing something after baptism. And after baptism means on the basis of baptism. You cannot impose a joined-up line which says, "Yes, we welcome you to new life in Christ; yes, we do trust your family to nourish you; but, no, we don't trust you with the bread of life." '

'Bishop, what changes have you noticed in the diocese?'

'We started this back in 1998. So seven or so years on we have a number of parishes where this is now normal practice. It's grown methodically and carefully, and much more slowly than I would have liked. I didn't feel, despite having put it through the General Synod, that as Chairman of the Liturgical Commission I should be pushing this with rites specifically with children in mind, but now as I leave the Commission this is very much at the top of my agenda. What's changed most is that those congregations that meet not necessarily in the traditional parish church mode, but in the church school after the school day on a time other than a Sunday, are celebrating the Eucharist again. The children bring along their friends and become evangelists because of their enthusiasm and sense of belonging to something special. That's the thing that seems to be new as we think about new forms of building church – what's called Mission Shaped Church or Fresh Expressions these days – and the more I think about these kinds of contexts in which some of the baptized, be they children, teachers, parents, governors, whatever, or others in a different context, the more they have a kind of infectious enthusiasm for their faith, the more people in their peer groups are naturally drawn into it.

'That's also true in our diocesan link with the Sudan; when you go there you are simply bowled over by their enthusiasm for their faith and their delight in doing it. Children there will sing and dance in the African moonlight for hours without stopping: it's mind-blowing to Westerners who always seem so bored and blasé.'

'Finally, Bishop, having guided the Church through the introduction of Common Worship *and as you stand down from the Liturgical Commission, where do you see us going next?'*

'We do have to ask ourselves if the Eucharistic patterns and rites we now have are right for that kind of dynamic all-age focus, especially where the special, irregular service is becoming significant enough to challenge the regular worshipping pattern of the community. I think there is always an opportunity to see how the community that is becoming church can and should best celebrate the Eucharist. This means addressing the context in which it is celebrated and taking seriously the question of who is the celebrant. It's the community – the whole community. I think that more important to me than working out how we can enable children to join in the celebration of an adult Eucharist is how children can help us become a whole Eucharistic community of the baptized.

'When I was a school chaplain in the 1970s and we used to celebrate late-night communion services, the teenagers would contribute a great deal to what was then viewed as the highly dangerous and experimental Series Three; nonetheless, the way they would choose readings, want to do question and answer after the readings, the way they wanted to introduce bits of intercession into the Eucharistic Prayer in order to put people in their thoughts at the heart of the church's prayer, made the act of worship come alive for them. That whole kind of experience needs to be re-imagined now with children who are by nature habitual worshippers and people of prayer, and who haven't yet fallen into the cynicism (or peer-pressured cynicism) of teenage years. Involving children in the celebration of the Eucharist in a real sense – not just bringing them into church from their classes to receive the sacrament – will change our worship, and formulating that worship for the use of the whole Church will be an exciting project to undertake. That's what the Commission has a chance to do next.'

Interview 2
Children and the Church
Diana Murrie
National Children's Officer (until mid 2006)

Diana is a children's advocate; her enthusiasm for the place of children in the life of the Church is powerful. Full of anecdotes, she travelled up and down the country helping parishes and specialist groups to see the importance of effective ministry among children. Diana is the best friend the children of the Church of England have got. As the Church of England National Children's Officer she worked collaboratively with the network of Diocesan Children's Work Advisers in training and resourcing diocesan clergy and laity in their delivery of best-quality, appropriate worship and nurture programmes for children in parishes. She was previously the Bristol Diocesan Children and Junior Youth Adviser, and prior to this present post was Head of Prayer and Spirituality at the Mothers' Union in Mary Sumner House. The following interview was conducted while Diana was still the National Children's Officer.

'Diana, with new guidance now available within the Church, what do you want to be saying to parishes at this time?'

'Parishes now have to look at children and communion. Rather than say "We don't want this" or "This doesn't apply to us", parishes are more and more aware that they have to say to themselves, from the point of view of their mission and ministry, "How are we going to best support a child who has already had permission to receive in a previous parish and who turns up in our church on a Sunday?" You can't reject them; we all have to be ready now. How would we feel about not being ready for an adult visitor? This child is a member of the Body of Christ. It's like saying we don't need fire insurance because we've never had a fire. One of the interesting things at the moment is new work in looking at the theology of childhood; what is childhood for? The fact that God became child; God was inside Mary for nine months – why? Why not just have him arrive like Elijah, striding across the stage, why this emphasis on childhood all the way through? Why have nativity narratives if there is not a purpose? Children and women are affirmed throughout the Gospels. Adults throughout the Gospels are urged to change, children are not; in fact adults are urged to become like a child in order to enter the Kingdom of Heaven. Now why, what is this? There has to be a reason. There seems to have been nowhere to put this theological work. Yet it's there in scripture and out there in real life, where children are.

'Ann Richards has famously said, "Children help us to remember that which we've forgotten." So if a parish engages with this subject of children and communion it will discover that this is a process of renewal and important for the spiritual life of the church. At the end of the day, even if a congregation decide in all openness and learning that this is not for them, fine, but they still have to be ready not to exclude communicant children who move into the area. In those places where there are no children, they should agree to revisit the subject in a couple of years, for surely the status quo in such places (i.e. no children present) should not be an on-going expectation. This is a moving thing, it isn't going to go away.'

'People would expect the National Children's Officer to be in favour of this, but how does it influence you personally?'

'Right the way back in my time in Sunday School, I used to think of growth in faith as a journey. But actually, now I see it more as a spiral staircase. The same things come around but we see them from a different perspective. It's like the Church's year, every time we engage with the mystery of that, hopefully there's a deeper insight. We need to do this with the Gospel narratives, because the Gospel narratives are often given to us as children and rarely taught again, yet they hold all we need.

'Too many of us in the Church have lost that awareness of the story through the challenges of adulthood. That's what so much of the material in courses like Alpha and Emmaus are doing, teaching again, or for the first time, the Gospel story. Many people coming to faith now have not been to Sunday School, so we can't take this for granted. It helps when preachers offer "wondering" questions in sermons. Children wonder. The preacher asks, "Where are you in this story?" and leaves the question hanging there. People come up afterwards very angry, wanting to be told what to think by the sermon, but actually our task is to think for ourselves and find ourselves in the revelation of Jesus.'

'*What can you tell us about the place of children in the Church as you see it?*'

'I'm no theologian but I'm told that the Greek word *logos* means "word" but it also can mean "reasoning", and because children didn't have words when they were young, they didn't have reasoning. In many early households, well-to-do households, there was a strict hierarchical structure with the father, then mother, then the senior servants in order. Children came below that, so that when people read Jesus' saying "Unless you become as a little child" it sounded insulting. Many New Testament scholars, though, would say that in fact children did receive communion in the early church because the Acts of the Apostles would have said that they were excluded, if they had been. There would not have been any ambiguity. This is particularly true when we read Acts 2.39: "For the promise is for you, for your children, for all who are far away, everyone whom the Lord our God calls to him." This is inclusive and does not just refer to children as potential people still to come, but here and now. At no point does it say, "except the children".

'In the story of the travels of Egeria (the fourth-century nun who wrote about early Christian Jerusalem) we read of children being put on the shoulders of the adults to be able to see, so we know that children were present at these early gatherings. In the Gospels themselves, the fact that it was a child who brought the food to Jesus for the feeding of the five thousand is significant. The adults have no answer but in all innocence and enthusiasm a child provides what Jesus needs. He is not bothered that it's inadequate, he doesn't know what Jesus is going to do with it, he just offers it. He says to himself, "Jesus wants something and I've got it and he can have it." So we can see, if we're open enough, that the Christian understanding of the place of children is, or should be, one not only of equality but also of revelation.'

'So where does that take us, Diana?'

'Where it takes us is often uncomfortable. Things like: so Jesus takes bread and says, "This is my body" – that is sacrament; Jesus takes wine and says, "This is my blood" – that is sacrament; Jesus takes the child and says this is the Kingdom – is that sacrament? The child is given as a model for the Christian life, it's as simple as that, and often we don't like it. But the even more radical thing is that children don't know that they've got this gift, which embodies this very point. For adults, the challenge is not to see children as empty vessels but actually seeing children as having something unique and essential for heaven. This is the definition of being "born again"; we may not realize it but becoming like the child is part of the birth pangs of the new age. It's looking at childhood as a blueprint for the Christian life for us all.'

'So where does this leave the Church of England? What's your overview?'

'Well, I hesitate to say this but we must be careful that confirmation is working. It must not become the Sunday School leaving certificate. You see, what happens is that children, while they're young, are open to question and wonder, but gradually children can become excluded from the worshipping life of the church, as they are sent out to Sunday School or whatever it's called and they never find their place again. This whole thing, children and communion, is about holding and growing children into the life of the church, it's not just about a cut-off point to be reached.

'In real terms, we have children and adults in the church by real good fortune. I think what's happening in reality – and it's just anecdotal – is that in churches that are nurturing children as people in their own right they tend to be known by their Christian names rather than as Jane's children or the Sub Dean's children or David's family or whatever. Children must be part of the whole congregation, and confirmation must be about the public ownership of this membership for them. Perhaps children need to choose when Confirmation is right for them.'

'How has the progress of children and communion been way-marked for you as an adviser on children's work in the Church?'

'If you look back in detail at the motion brought to the General Synod in 2000 all was nearly lost. Well-meaning per-haps, but the motion suggested that everybody in the Church should do this, or nobody should. I maintain that if everybody had been made to do this, it would not have grown as a vibrant life-giving experience within the Church. What if we'd said that about the ordination of women? I remember a bish-op coming up to me at the time and saying, "I can't stop this, it's grown too far." For example, in 1993 we wrote to all the bishops and in every diocese we found examples of children receiving communion. This was a growing pastoral practice and of course in the Anglican Communion as a whole it has become the norm. Where the practice of children and com-munion exists, its take-up is 100 per cent. It is an organic pro-cess, like a growing plant. It needs support and pruning but it will, in time, stand by itself despite regulations that in essence are more for the benefit of adults rather than children. To fur-ther the analogy, it can be a prickly plant for some, but it is a plant that flowers. Children and communion asks questions of yourself and your church and it will not wither.'

'This issue was given to the people on the ground to progress, people like individual clergy and diocesan children's advisers, and now it has come full circle. We know this to be an important issue and only now is the Church ready to engage with it. It brings with it the opening up of baptism in terms of understanding and the equipping of clergy and others to be able to talk about faith as a source of growth in communion with God. Ministerial training needs to include time on the theology of childhood and key ways of understanding the Gospel texts to bring them alive for all ages. Children are not a problem, they are a gift, co-workers in the Gospel.'

'Do you have a last line, on behalf of the children of the Church of England?'

'Yes: think about it, what does it mean to you to play in the Kingdom of God?'

Interview 3
Evangelicals and children and communion
Mark Russell
Member of Archbishops' Council

Mark is deeply engaged in ministry among children and young people. He is charismatic, warm and intelligent. As a lay person he brings to the Church vibrancy and clarity that are to be cherished. He is currently Youth Minister at Christ Church, Chorleywood. He read Law at Queen's University in Belfast, and was admitted as a fully accredited local preacher in the Methodist Church in Ireland in 1996 and as a reader in the Church of England in 2002. Mark has worked in industrial management, and as a youth pastor of a Methodist Church in Northern Ireland. He was a recipient of the 'Tomorrow's People' award in 1999 for his commitment to building peace among young people in Northern Ireland. Mark has travelled across England, and internationally, as a Christian speaker to young people. In 2005, General Synod confirmed his appointment to the Archbishops' Council. He has been selected for ordination training and has recently been appointed Chief Executive Officer of the Church Army.

'Mark, why is the area of children and communion important to you?'

'It's close to my heart very strongly because I think it's something the Church hasn't addressed properly. I think many churches see communion as purely for adults and patronize children, and I think that too many adults don't understand that many, many children and young people have very committed relationships with God and want to know Jesus Christ better. I remember an eight-year-old who, when I asked him what, for him, was important about communion, said, "'Cause I feel Jesus Christ inside me." Now I've not heard a better definition of Eucharistic theology than that in my entire life. So it's important to me because I think these kids know the Lord. If we believe as Anglicans in infant baptism, then on what other journey do you not give them their first meal until they're a teenager, and for well over a decade they're starving? I see communion very much as the nourishing meal of the whole Body of Christ and to exclude one part of that because of their age is wrong.'

'Coming from Northern Ireland and a different background, has this been a process of discovery for you?'

'I come from a Methodist background so the view of sacraments is quite low, so to move into the Anglican setting where the view of sacraments is quite high has caused me to think through exactly what this means. To be perfectly frank, I think my understanding of communion has heightened since being in the Church of England rather than being back home. Its importance and centrality to worship and discipleship has become clearer, and so because of my work with children and young people I've learnt that children and youth worship is not a baby-sitting service: it's not simply there to provide something sweet and lovely for the kids while the parents are in proper church, it's actually helping these young people to grow in faith themselves and helping them to discover God's love for them. Ultimately God's love is given to us in Jesus Christ, in his body and blood. Therefore I do feel, very strongly, that communion is the meal of the whole family of God, the meal of the whole Body; so provided someone understands what they're doing – actually I'm not sure I agree with that now I've said it – provided people know what they're doing has real significance then I'm very happy for children to receive it.

'One of the comments that came up recently in General Synod was that "children shouldn't receive communion because they don't understand it". This gives me the chance to correct what I said a moment ago. I'm not sure I fully understand at the time, in fact I don't understand it very often to be honest, that God's love is so graciously poured out for me. There's an element of mystery that we've lost out on – perhaps that's something the Catholic tradition can teach us Evangelicals, this idea of awe and wonder. So my qualification for communion is that if somebody wants to know Jesus better, communion is an essential part of that knowing.'

'So, Mark, how is this reflected in the practice at Chorleywood?'

'Well, we have a lot of children and young people. For the children up to the age of around ten or eleven, they tend to meet on Sunday mornings, in parallel to the main morning service. They come in near the end and either they come up with their group and they receive a blessing or they return to their families and receive communion alongside them. So we're placing a responsibility on parents to decide whether children are in the right place to start receiving communion. And if that is the case what happens is that the minister gives the bread to the parent who then shares that appropriately with their child. In the evening the presumption is the opposite. This tends to be attended by the older children and young people. There the presumption is that all receive communion unless they choose not to. Our understanding is that if a young person is baptized and wanting to know and love Jesus better, in Christ Church it's an open table and they're welcome to receive.'

'What do you think about the question of a minimum age for this?'

'I would argue that it's impossible to set an arbitrary age. I know some children under seven years old who have a phenomenal faith in God, who tell me that God speaks to them when they pray, who ask me questions about the Trinity, who ask me questions about the Bible. I have no question in my mind whatsoever that these younger people are exploring their faith and they are as much a part of God's Kingdom as I am, so I don't think you can draw an age limit. I know what some bishops have tried to do and it's been part of the developing process, but I just don't think it's possible to do this with a number. The Guidelines are, deliberately, non age specific. I think that's very important. All that's important for me is that children have some comprehension of what's going on around them and that parents, with the help and support of church staff, are the best ones to make that decision.'

'Mark, what can you tell then about the place of Confirmation and how children and young people grow in the faith from your experience?'

'I guess my experience today with young people is that young people's discipleship with Jesus Christ is less Damascus

Road and more Emmaus Road. There are Damascus Road moments, there are radical moments of change, but my experience with the hundreds of young people I've worked with is that it's a period of progression and growth. The church ought to be a community of discernment and so what we're trying to do is to give people a place where they can come and belong and not necessarily sign up to anything, and come and have safety, belong, ask questions, watch, observe, and through that discover God's love for them, and that's been our method. So youth work is really on the cutting edge as I think that's what the adult church is going to have to become more and more than it is at present.

'So what we've discovered over recent years is that young people will often come in on the fringes, brought in by someone else, and will slowly move more and more into the centre until finally the light comes on and they all realize what a wonderful thing is happening. If at any point along that journey we were to say "No", then that would put shutters in the way and that would be exclusive, unwelcoming and would not work. It all depends on what you see Confirmation as. Confirmation is not a topping up of Baptism, and Bishops need to understand that. Baptism is the point of entry into the Christian Church. Confirmation is membership of the Church and a public ownership of faith.

'Perhaps equally significantly, and this is something Evangelicals don't push too often because we're quite happy with the confessional strand, is that it is God confirming us, saying "I love you", "I think you're incredible", "I'm confirming you in my love". As Rowan Williams put it once when referring to John 14, "It's discovering your little room in God's love." It's a phrase that has resonated with me. So our practice is that Confirmation is a marker on the road, a significant moment and important. We believe in it, we had thirty-six candidates last year: these people don't just pop out of the woodwork, these are people who have come along and want to discover more. Confirmation ought never to be seen as a gateway to communion, it's a gateway to discipleship. It's not a ticket to communion, it's not a passport stamp and it's important that we recognize that.'

'How do you think young people see receiving communion today?'

'I think young people perceive this as being very important; the problem is that in some quarters when young people are excluded in any way then the church appears unwelcoming and that young people aren't part of the Body of Christ, and then it's a turn off. You know I've said this before: we do youth work not because we're passionately concerned that the Church of England won't be here in twenty years; we don't do youth work because the adults who come to church have kids who need embracing in their own sub-culture; we do youth work because we are passionately committed that God loves younger people and loves them as much as he loves adults and that the church is frankly, incomplete without them.

'*Mission-shaped Church* has a sentence in it which I've committed to memory because it's so scary: "Over half the churches of England have virtually no engagement with young people; worse still, most of us accept that fact with relative indifference." To me, opening communion to children and young people will not be the panacea for that problem but what it is doing is making another statement that children and young people are a key and integral part of the Church of England and that we should see them as part of what we do and who we are. Only then will we be an authentic church.'

'So is it too strong to say that this could be a matter of justice then for children and young people?'

'Well, it's ironic that the very meal that Jesus instituted to be a symbol of unity, a symbol of togetherness, is often the thing that divides us the most. I love the fact that the word is "remember", because it is "re-membering" the Body of Christ, for at the moment it's not. Communion is vital for that. I've always been an advocate for children and young people being seen as equals in God's Kingdom. So for Evangelical parishes who haven't yet made this a priority I say, "Make it one, it's where we're at." The Church has failed children and young people for generations and they have voted with their feet. This Church is losing young people, haemorrhaging them massively.

'If you ask young people they'll tell you they perceive the Church to be old-fashioned, unwelcoming and adult orientated. Once I was in a high school doing an assembly and I asked the young people to throw words at me which they thought described the Church of England, and all those descriptions came out: old, grey, boring, out of touch, old-fashioned, dusty buildings. But then one word came that hit me and scared the life out of me, and the word was "irrelevant". Of all the things that we are we shouldn't be irrelevant: surely the most relevant message that anyone has to offer is "God loves you."

'I heard a story, not in this country, of an Anglican priest who went into a school and celebrated Communion according to the 1662 service and then said, "Anyone who is entitled to receive should come forward," and that turned out to be him, one member of staff and one pupil, and the other three hundred kids and staff had to just watch.

'That's how not to do it. Again it's just about making church accessible: clergy need to grasp this issue, PCCs need to grasp this issue, leadership teams need to grasp this issue, and to Evangelical parishes that say "No", I'd ask them to go back and read their Bible again. We need to read in the Gospels where Jesus embraced children and welcomed them. What he actually said was unless you receive the Kingdom of God as a child, you'll not enter it. The evidence is compelling.'

'Can you say a bit more about how Evangelicals should look at this issue?'

'The point is, I understand a number of Evangelical colleagues may have reservations with this and it's tied up with the confessional strand again, but I actually think that children can do the confessional strand if they're allowed to do it and if it's explained to them in language they'll understand: they'll happily make that confession of faith, probably much more readily than adults would, and they have a much more open faith than we have. Now from an Evangelical perspective, Evangelicals ought to be known for their commitment to the authority of scripture, and as far as I'm concerned, reading scripture, reading the Gospels, it's pretty clear that Jesus loved kids and he saw them as equal. Jesus welcomed people that society didn't take very seriously: women were one example and the other were children, and both were told that they had central roles in his Kingdom.

'Jesus was right, children have a gift, they have a perception of things that adults don't have. I remember a little guy came up to me one Sunday and said, "Mark, God told me to tell you you're too busy." Now that child spoke into my life in a way no adult ever has, or had the nerve to, and I don't doubt for a second that that was God's word to me that Sunday morning.

'The other thing I'd add for the importance of children being admitted to communion is that the Church is so frequently (and we from Evangelical quarters are particularly guilty of this) a cerebral affair. It's all words, all about words, whether we pray them or say them; there's not a lot of time for silence, there's not a lot of time for symbolism, and this generation understand symbols, they understand things they can see and touch, and Jesus must have understood that too because ultimately Communion is about seeing, touching, tasting and seeing that the Lord is good. That's also very culturally relevant.

'I see particularly in friends of mine from the Catholic tradition who've done a "Youth Eucharist", and coming as I do from a Northern Irish Protestant background we would have thought that this was the worst possible kind of youth service, but actually I've come to see, from working in this country and working in the C of E, that young people relate to that because it's something they can see and touch, and for this generation that's real.'

'So, we've talked about different traditions, as a member of the Archbishops' Council, do you see this as a way forward for the Church of England?'

'Yes, it is. I'm on record as having said this both in Archbishops' Council and in General Synod, that the Church of England says it is very committed to working with children and young people. We agree that in principle, but when it comes to practicalities, when it comes to changing individual practices and traditions, when it comes to putting money in, then we're less committed than we sound. I believe passionately that this is the meal that unifies the Body of Christ and I think it is exciting to think what God can do with this, if we have the nerve, if we have the faith and if we have the confidence to be bold.

'I think also that this is a prophetic statement to children and young people, that we see you as part of this Church, we're not going to bus you out to the next room to colour something in while the adults have communion. We're going to have you as a key and integral part of the community of faith that meets in this place. Of course, and this is an unusual thing for an Evangelical to say, in the priestly function of presiding at the Lord's Table he or she represents much more than that little parish or that little village, but represents the fact that this is the meal of the entire catholic body, the Church universal.

'Suddenly you buy into that, you're part of it, you're part of this massive pilgrim people that started with Jesus Christ two thousand years ago, has walked through these years, and you're still part of that process, part of that journey. Ultimately, for me and what I teach young people is that this is a walk with Jesus who walks beside us, and with Communion he's within us, and when you're on a journey you need nourishment. So for me, Communion is the nourishing meal for the pilgrim walk with Jesus Christ.'

'If this is so important, we need to prepare for worship and involvement in worship more deeply. What would you say from your experience about how the Church should work towards this? It's fine for those of us in big churches but what about those with few resources and where professional ministry is at a premium?'

'One of the trendy terms in ministry today is co-operation and collaboration: now what does that mean? It means in worship involving people of all ages, in leading, praying, reading, helping to distribute. One of my vicar's friends, when it comes to asking his bishop for permission to administer the Eucharistic elements, proposes his entire Electoral Roll, because if you're part of the community you should be just that and this is a sign of that membership. We try to involve people as much as we possibly can but that takes more effort and time, it involves phone calls, it requires you to take risks and, more than that, it requires you to hand over control. Clergy, and I guess all of us in leadership, aren't very good at doing that. A few months ago I was preparing a service and I asked a young man of fourteen years old to preach for us. He doesn't have a Bishop's Licence of course, so I told the Bishop, and he smiled; so the lad preached. Before he got up to speak, I pulled him to one side and said, "Whatever happens next I'm really proud of you, the fact is you've had the courage to do this and whatever happens

I'm really proud of you, Josh." He goes, "Mark, I'm not remotely concerned about this; if I make a hash of this the Vicar will kick your ass, not mine!" And this was right; I was responsible for the service and he was right.

'So preparation is crucial because this isn't just a priest-driven thing but actually it's the whole community driving it. That's risky, and it can be messy at times, but, you know what, that's the Christian life, isn't it? That's authentic and that's real. There have been so many occasions where, as a professional, I've thought "Oh my goodness" or "That's terrible" when leading worship and yet people come up to me afterwards and say, "That was an incredible service", because they've been involved, it felt real.

'Of course there are times, especially if you work with children and young people, that it will feel like chaos – you will get occasional chaos, but that's life. So be bold, look out on Sunday morning and ask who can be involved, who can lead and encourage young and old to take part. And by the way, it's more fun! Some time ago we were supposed to have an open air service but the weather was awful so we were genuinely in chaos. An older member of the congregation, who normally came to the more traditional early service, came along, and when he came to speak to me I was dreading the comment. He said, "I have not seen so much life in this church for over fifty years. Thank you." That's what I mean.'

'So sum up your thought for me, Mark. Why welcome children to communion?'

'The bigger picture for the Church of England is that it is welcoming children and young people into the Church in a real way. It sees them as equals, as co-disciples, following Jesus. Children are not the church of tomorrow; they are the church of today without whom there will be no church of tomorrow.'

Interview 4
Stephen Venner
Bishop of Dover in Canterbury

Bishop Stephen has been fully involved in the promotion of children and communion for many years. He is a skilled chairman of the General Synod and an experienced pastor and leader. As Bishop of Dover he has care for the Diocese of Canterbury while the Archbishop fulfils his other duties. He has been Bishop of Dover since 1999, which means that he is in practice the Diocesan Bishop for Canterbury, exercising that ministry on behalf of the Archbishop. He and his wife Judy (an Education Adviser for Kent County Council) live in Canterbury.

Earlier, Stephen was a parish priest for twenty-five years, serving in inner-city South London, on a large housing estate in Wiltshire, and in an established 'civic' church in Dorset. In 1994 Stephen was ordained Bishop of Middleton, responsible for the Metropolitan Boroughs of Rochdale, Oldham and Tameside in the Diocese of Manchester.

Education is very much in the blood, and Stephen is a trained teacher. He is Vice-Chairman of the Church of England's Board of Education, serves on a range of national educational committees, has chaired three diocesan Boards of Education, and is Pro-Chancellor (Chairman of Governors) of Canterbury Christ Church University.

He has been actively involved in the follow-up to *Children in the Way*, and was a member of the teams which produced *All God's Children?* and *ON the WAY*. In recent years, Stephen has piloted the General Synod's discussions and decisions regarding admitting children to Holy Communion before Confirmation.

In addition to many other responsibilities, Bishop Stephen serves on the Kent Strategic Partnership, representing the Christian communities of Kent.

'Bishop, you've been involved in the development of children receiving communion before confirmation for many years. Where do you see that we are now?'

'I think we've been through a period of years where the whole subject has been something that only enthusiasts have been interested in, people interested in particular in children and the liturgy, but I think it's gradually moving on now so that more and more parishes are beginning to realize that this is a subject they ought to consider. Also, bishops who've been a bit ambivalent about it are beginning to say a few encouraging words to their children's advisers and education staff, rather than the issue being reduced to another lobby or at worse just being ignored in the hope it will go away.'

'You opened the debate in the July 2005 General Synod; can you expand on the need to bring the Guidelines to a more formal basis?'

'There are two different aspects of that: one of the things that delighted me about the debate was that it was the first time we've had a debate on the issue in Synod that's been taking it for granted that it's happening and that it's growing. Up to now it's been "Should we allow it?" or "Should we pull the plug on it?" Five years ago when the Diocese of Bristol put its motion, it really was a negative motion, with a view that we should all stop. Now there is hardly a voice heard except in support. There were cautions around and that's very appropriate, but the spirit was "We are doing this and we are going to continue doing this; let's talk about how it's best done."

'Then the other aspect is the canonical issue. Bishop Colin Buchanan has said for several years that the way the Church has been operating is not the right legal way forward. Up till now we've been working under the Canon which says that we can admit "those that are willing and desirous to be confirmed" and so on. Colin's valuable insight is that the whole point of inviting children to receive Holy Communion is that they are not yet ready to make that commitment of faith which is part of Confirmation. This is advice the Church has largely ignored until now; further on in that Canon we can move forward under regulation from the House of Bishops, so that puts it on a legal footing. This is clearly a more appropriate way, but it requires Regulations rather than Guidelines.'

'Your last post was Bishop of Middleton in Manchester Diocese, one of the dioceses with experimental permission. How would you compare and contrast the experience there with what you found in Canterbury Diocese?'

'Different time, different spirit. Manchester led the way as they did with so many other things but it was patchy in the early days. There were a few places that did it but it didn't feature powerfully on the diocesan agenda. There certainly wasn't a drive to it, it was simply that permission was given and it happened. Parishes would approach the Board of Education for advice (the proper place I think to place this issue). In Canterbury the situation was that Archbishop Carey had been prepared for this to happen but his heart was not really in it, so that although there were places in the diocese where children were allowed to receive communion there were not very many, and often only where the incumbent had a real passion for it.

'When I discovered this situation, we began to change the model and our children's adviser has been instructed to be rather more proactive. But I think the major difference is that we're now in a situation where enough parishes in the Diocese of Canterbury and around the country are doing it to allow us to say to parishes that may just be beginning to consider it, "Go and talk to Parish X down the road." I increasingly believe that parishes who want to take this step of faith would like to talk to somebody who's already done it in order to learn the lessons beforehand. So there will be some centres of excellence around the place and some places that have learned the lessons the hard way.'

'These places which have tackled children and communion already, are they larger, more urban type parishes?'

'I think probably not. I think it's many of the smaller ones who have a small number of children, whom everybody knows, who are very much part of the congregation, where the whole people of God feel it's totally unfair on children to be brought to the communion rail and denied the meal of this community. They are all fellow worshippers Sunday by Sunday. The larger parishes often see the organizational problems of the children, while out doing their obviously important work in Sunday School, having to modify their activity and come back into the service. At what point children should return is another issue that actually can act as a disincentive. But the practice is growing and parishes of all shapes and sizes are increasingly looking to grow in this way.'

'Bishop, is there a churchmanship issue here at all? How would you describe the possible debate between believing versus belonging as a caricature of any such divide?'

'I'd answer this in a slightly different way I think. I was talking to a very evangelically minded person recently and she was saying that she was not really in favour of children making their communion before confirmation because they didn't "fully understand". When I said that I didn't fully understand either she was quite taken aback and we quickly got into a discussion about the nature of the Eucharist; she coming from the point of view that it was solely a commemoration of an event that happened in the past and making it real in our lives, and me arguing the real presence of Jesus both in Word and Sacrament. I further believe she had never been involved in the administration of Holy Communion, and I think that anybody who has been so involved only has to look into the faces of children to realize that they understand this in a far more profound way than most adults. There is a real sense that this is an awesome and wonder-full experience.

'So it is that I feel very strongly that children making their communion when they're still very young are a real gift to the adults in the congregation. This whole subject is more of a gift to the adults than it is to the children. Adults, in an English tradition, can sort of "take it or leave it". We all know that behaviour in church while you're waiting for communion and while people are coming back leaves a certain something to be desired – of course in other dioceses and other parishes! Adults have only got to look at the way in which children receive communion to be brought up short and to realize the innocence they have lost.'

'How do you see the new Regulations working in the future?'

'I think the new Regulations are important but are secondary to the basic principle which seems to be fundamental to the way in which we are church. Do we believe as a worshipping community that children are fully paid-up, active members of our worshipping communities whom we cannot do without? Or do we really believe that they are merely "potential" Christians who in due course, with lots of training and teaching, will be able to take their place with us as adult members of the congregation? I actually think it's as fundamental as that. When I was in Weymouth as a parish priest I had one of those disclosure moments. One Sunday I stood up in front of the congregation to say in the normal way, "We are the Body of Christ. In the one Spirit we were all baptized into one body. Let us then pursue all that makes for peace and builds up our common life," announced the Offertory Hymn and then the children came in. I suddenly thought to myself, "What on earth are we doing?" And so we changed our order, even though it is not in the rubrics. The hymn came first during which the children came in and the first words everyone then heard were "We are the Body of Christ," because now we were and before we were incomplete.'

'*What do you think about minimum age limits, Bishop?*'

'If I were pushed I would opt to give children communion from baptism much as the Orthodox Church does. However, in current practice we are really looking at the children being of an age when they can sit down with their parents, or their priest or a member of the congregation, ideally some combination of those persons, and begin to discover something of this special and holy sacrament. The Regulations are non age specific because they are concerned with process rather than age, and what is appropriate for that congregation and those children. When it comes to pastoral practice, such as parents breaking a wafer for a young child, then I think that there are certain places where it is foolish for us to tread. On those occasions, it is an act of sheer love; they have received grace and love from Jesus and their natural, appropriate, parental instinct is to want to share that with their children. I just think it is very inappropriate for any rules, regulations or even priests to interfere with this very proper and holy expression of love. I believe in a God who is big enough to cope with this, so we should err on the side of generosity and allow God to do his stuff with his beloved people.'

'*Bishop, with your experience on the Board of Education and having been involved in teaching and learning for many years, what would you say about how children learn and the importance of spiritual development?*'

'In the National Curriculum there is a growing awareness that spiritual development is an essential part of the whole learning process. It's described in various neutral terms such as awe and wonder. My wife, who is an education adviser, remembers a particular class she was in one day. The teacher was busy teaching and then a butterfly flew in through the open window. The children all immediately started looking at the butterfly. The teacher told the children to concentrate on the subject because it was important. At the end of the lesson Judy and the teacher talked about the missed opportunity of reflecting on the wonder of this creature in their midst.

There's a place in north Italy called Reggio Emelia where post-war they decided to put the money they had into rebuilding their community. The focus for their funding was pre-school education and there they have tremendous work that is certainly spiritual if not overtly religious. It encourages teachers to spend time with the children, exploring the world of ideas. So, for example, in our schools, if the children have painted a face, say in half an hour, these Italian children will spend three weeks painting eyes! You can imagine these small children discovering the many worlds of eyes: happy eyes, sad eyes, or perplexed eyes. We can only imagine what this is doing for these children and their sense of the world and people around them. In the Church, we need such ideas to open the eyes of our children to the wonder of the love Jesus has for them, especially in Holy Communion, and to begin to see him, as we all should, in every person and every situation.'

'As a Bishop, how do you engage with this thinking as you visit parishes?'

'When I arrived in the Diocese of Canterbury I went round every single parish and as I was talking to them I said, among other things, "Tell me about your worship." The vast majority of parishes said that they had a Parish Communion as the main service on Sundays and a monthly family service, sometimes Eucharistic, usually not. They would then go on to tell me about the family type service, describing the group that spends time together to prepare the service, choosing carefully the music, drama, readings and so on. All said it was really good and that numbers were considerably greater on these Sundays. "How do you prepare for the other Sundays?" I asked. They almost all said that then they just have an ordinary Communion service, or some comment of that kind. Looking over my spectacles I would reply along the lines of "How can a communion service ever be ordinary?" The point is about preparation and expectation.

'In more theoretical terms, when you talk to people about their work with children and young people, the phrase I hear more often than not is that we don't have a communion because that puts people off and they find it boring. Now you could not have a more multi-media, multi-faceted, all-embracing act than the Holy Communion, provided it is done with commitment, expertise and some sense of the wonder it was given to describe. So what I'm looking for from clergy in particular is making the Eucharistic experience that converting ordinance of which Wesley spoke which makes people come in and say "Wow and I'm part of this and isn't it wonderful"; and that's why we ought to be doing communions in schools also, for the same reasoning. We need to make this come to life as only the Eucharist can; simple things like drawing the children around the altar in order to be around and part of that central act of taking, blessing, breaking, sharing, has an enormous impact not only on the children but also on the adults in their pews who can see, on the outside as it were, the children's faces, the impact this ought to have in all our lives. God is there waiting to meet us. We should do all we can to open eyes, ears, noses, minds and hearts to him.'

'Bishop Stephen, what is your hope for the Church with the new regulations?'

'Last year, in at least eight dioceses of the Church of England, there were more children worshipping in church than in the previous year. Wouldn't it be wonderful if that were true of every diocese? Children and Holy Communion can only encourage the Church to grow. My hope is that we can all grow together and discover more of God's love for his people, so that we can be used by God to bring others to know of his love. And the best missionaries to children are children!'

Interview 5
Margaret Withers
Archbishop's Officer for Evangelism
with Children

Margaret Withers has been on the front line of ministry with children for many years. She has played a key role in the development of the Church of England's Strategy for Children.

Margaret Withers trained at the Royal College of Music and taught in several inner London schools and for the Open University before becoming a Diocesan Children's Adviser for Rochester in 1989. Her interest in liturgy and work as a parish organist led her to provide encouragement and training for parishes to involve children in services, especially all-age Eucharistic worship. In 1992, she set up the After School Club Project to provide training, funding and support to enable parishes to reach children through mid-week clubs.

While Children's Officer for the Diocese of Chelmsford, Margaret responded to the decision to admit children to Holy Communion before confirmation by writing a handbook and course, *Welcome to the Lord's Table*, which was first published in 1999 (see Appendix 2). She followed this with *The Gifts of Baptism* (Bible Reading Fellowship) in 2003.

Margaret was appointed the Archbishop's Officer for Evangelism among Children in June 2001. Her role includes providing encouragement, training and information and led to the publication of advice for churches wishing to develop their outreach among children, *Not Just Sunday* (2002) and *Where Two or Three . . .* (2004), both published by Church House Publishing.

Where Are the Children?, a major exploration of the issues and practicalities of the Church's ministry among children in the community, was published in February 2005.

'Margaret, you're known not only for your current post but also for your writing of one of the most popular preparation courses. How did you become involved in the move towards children receiving communion in the life of the Church?'

'Well, Chelmsford, where I was Children's Adviser, was one of the first dioceses to take on board that children could be admitted to Holy Communion. We had three initial meetings, one in each Episcopal area, and I expected to get about thirty people there, but we were packed out with up to one hundred and fifty people present at each. There were questions about all sorts of things, theological and pastoral questions of real interest. And people were also giving insights from other churches in the Anglican Communion, saying how it had transformed their life together. One lady of West Indian origin stood up with great style and proclaimed, "I rejoice that this is happening!"

'Then we started going around the parishes and I soon came to realize that different parishes would move at different speeds on this one and that we needed to be sensitive to that. I realized that many members of the Church of England saw Confirmation as being at the core of their sacramental life, so that Baptism wasn't complete until you were confirmed, and so receiving communion was therefore linked to Confirmation in this powerful but confusing way. It was a challenge to take this on board for many people. So I prepared several short teaching leaflets which proved to be the foundation stones of *Welcome to the Lord's Table*. So that document was born out of preparation and real experience with the parishes of the diocese. We need to be aware that if children are admitted to Holy Communion it will alter everything you do in your church.'

'Your job title uses the word "evangelism". How do children come to faith?'

'It's not just children. Admitting children to communion changes a church because the worshipping community has to engage with issues around the meaning of Baptism for us all, the place of children as part of the Church, about discernment of the sacrament rather than just cognitive understanding. Preaching and teaching about these subjects is so important here. When people say of children, "Will they understand? Will they behave?" I reply, "When you went forward to receive Communion on Sunday, did you understand? What were you thinking? Did you feel you were worthy because of your ability to articulate this deep mystery?" We all need to grow continually in discovering faith in Jesus.'

'So how does this change a church in your experience?'

'If children are fully involved in the life of the Church, it's not just about giving something to them; it's about the ministry they give to us. Any church that takes children seriously and sees them as ministers will get a new vitality and sense of hope from those children. They are our hope for today and for the future. I remember some time ago picking up a Concordance and looking up the word "children", and I hadn't realized how often the lack of children is mentioned as a sign of tragedy. "There are no children in the street" and so on. No children means there is no hope and no future.'

'In terms of evangelism, then, how do we go about engaging with children?'

'In terms of reaching out, it's about the Church meeting children where they are and engaging with them and their culture. We have to become more skilled at communicating with children in a language they can understand. This is why schools can be such a wonderful model of an all-age worshipping community. We cannot say to children that they must be like the child I was fifty years ago. That's why I keep using the over-familiar but correct phrase, "where they are", for that means culturally, socially and physically.

'We're on a hiding to nothing if we think that just because we have a lovely family friendly service with a few nice hymns on a Sunday morning the children will come. There are many factors to life on a Sunday morning for families today: Sunday trading, sports events, separated families, weekend working and so on. Anyway it's not the biblical model; Jesus did not sit in the synagogue and wait for the people to come to him. He was out and about relating to people in stories to do with their daily lives, and that is where we need to be. All this makes us vulnerable and we don't like that, but it's necessary. I'm often asked, "How will we know that the children will stay faithful?" My answer is always that the same applies to us, clergy and all. Conversion is not a once and for all, we are in a relationship. We should not make demands of children that they would not take on for themselves or that are unrealistic in our terms either. There is no reason to give children less dignity than other humans, just because they are not in adulthood.

'For most children, the church is not at the centre of their lives but on the fringe. We need to be involved with those places and activities where they are at the centre so that we can at least have a chance to relate to them. This is about recognizing that the largest congregation clergy will face each week may be the school assembly or, just as importantly, the smaller group at

Brownies or Cubs where moving worship can take place – this is also "church". The door is open for us. Also, one of the biggest growth points in the Church is work with under fives, and it's not only that these children experience worship, but so do their parents who are often enquirers.'

'You mention age there, what would you say about the right age for receiving Communion?'

'If this doesn't sound too grand, I think the House of Bishops was very wise not to place a minimum age in the new Regulations. There is no magic level but age does have to be taken seriously. We cannot have indiscriminate communion because it's too important for that. But once we have an arbitrary age set we are back into rejection. If it's seven, what about the child who is six and half and in the same class at school and in Sunday School? It must be about discernment and not about hurdles. I've had two children: my son wasn't confirmed until he was over fourteen because he said he wasn't ready to make the commitment; my daughter was bursting to receive Holy Communion from the earliest possible age. She was longing; every child is different. This can produce an interesting dynamic on a Sunday if there is all-age Eucharistic worship as there can be children present who are communicants but not some adults.

'For example, if you've got uniformed organizations and, say, some of the Brownies are receiving but their Leader is not a communicant, that makes nonsense of the age thing. Adults have the choice at the moment, children do not. Rules are all very well but we have to be flexible enough to enable evangelism to take place and to allow God to act. I remember working at a Roman Catholic school where there were strict rules about receiving the sacrament at the school Mass. One term, a young girl from a different faith background went forward to receive and was quizzed by the Head afterwards. Her response to the question why did she go forward was that she "wanted to be close to Jesus". She was duly baptized. The Church must not stand in the way.'

'*Margaret, can you say something about* Mission-shaped Church *and the place of children in this initiative?*'

'*Mission-shaped Church* couldn't include everything. This isn't meant to sound too critical but children seem only to be mentioned as passive beings. There's one sentence that says somewhere "twenty-five people and children". That one just hit me. It is of course an extremely good report but we must never take children for granted if we're going to be mission-shaped. I have therefore offered training and a commentary to add this important aspect. I want to look at the way in which children are part of a mission-shaped church. Children cannot be seen on the edge of the church. Often it's not deliberate, it just never occurs to us, too often. Jesus' teaching was that we need to be like little children, not for the children to become little adults. The disciples marginalized the children and he was angry with them.'

'*You've mentioned schools a number of times and meeting children there. Eucharistic ministry in schools demands a very real partnership between all those involved, priest, parish, school staff, children and parents. I think you have an example of good practice to share with me.*'

Margaret then introduced the Revd Antony Homer, Curate of Christ Church St Leonard's in the Diocese of Chichester, a parish at that time in interregnum. Margaret said, 'At Christ Church, they describe the school as a "distinctive Eucharistic community".'

'*Antony, can you describe this distinctive Eucharistic community?*'

'It's an extended Eucharistic community which forms the largest regular congregation of the week. What makes them distinct is that they are a community which loves and cares for each other the whole time. Children are prayer partners to each other; they are sponsors for each other. Each Lent we prepare for admission to Holy Communion several children. Their preparation consists of anointing, regular times of prayer and study and a performance of the Passiontide Gospel, the children receiving for the first time soon after Easter. The service is theirs; all I do is the Absolution, Eucharistic Prayer and the final Blessing. They even prepare the Eucharistic Prayer around a recognizable structure – they decide what they wish to give thanks to God for. It is a living, lively act of worship in which we all come together.'

'This sounds wonderful. How do you go about ministering in such an environment?'

'The first thing to say is that a priest needs to get in and kick a football about, be seen at breaktime, lunchtime and become known to the children. Equally, a priest needs to be a friend of the staffroom. Secure an open invitation, then drink their coffee and eat their biscuits. The greatest gift I ever had before ordination was to be called to be a teacher, but that isn't necessary to be able to do this well. I was a secondary teacher doing A-Levels, now I'm working with people who want to tie your shoelaces together! But this is priestly ministry not a teaching ministry, being there and being known and being approachable, a friend of the school. You have to be yourself; don't try to be anything other than who God has called you to be. I don't have kids so it's not that I have that experience to help me, this is for everyone. Be seen after school so that parents get to know you also. In the Eucharist, you do exactly as you would do for adults but in a way that the children will understand and engage with; and if you don't know what that is, ask them, they'll tell you with enthusiasm. Work with the staff, for they know best, and celebrate the school's life and share in its sorrows.'

'How does this relate to what you do in church on Sundays?'

'Well, we've just celebrated Harvest and we decided that the school would come, on a Sunday, and do what they do but in our context. This was going to be a challenge as our tradition is as firmly Anglo-Catholic as you can get and everything has to be done just so. Everything is sung and pivotal to the priest. If anything is out of place, it's noticed. This, though, was to be the children teaching the congregation, for education in developing worship is everything. I opened the service with the Greeting and a child welcomed the people. We'd spent ages preparing with the Head, the children, the Director of Music, the choir: children were servers and fully involved throughout. A child then called us to repentance, three children sang the penitential rite just as we do it Sunday by Sunday, we then had the Peruvian Gloria which some of our folk are now saying they prefer.

'One reading, Noah, then Psalm 139 was read with a solo flute playing, it was so moving. For the Gospel the children enacted the miraculous catch of fish, then small Keystage 1 children led the intercessions. This consisted of a PowerPoint presentation of photographs the children had taken of our local area, people on the street, people who needed help – it's a very deprived area – pictures of the seashore, fish, fishermen and so on. All this with a child's voice in a vast Victorian building. It was an utterly Catholic celebration of the Mass but it spoke to all. At the end we went in great procession down to bless the sea and came back for coffee. There were over four hundred people in church that day. Nearly two hundred people received Holy Communion, half of them children. It was utterly fabulous, we had no complaints, and it was the church gathering to worship in its fullest possible way.'

'And the comments?'

'We've had no negative comments that I'm aware of. In fact afterwards one of our elderly ladies who comes to Mass every day came to me with tears in her eyes and said, "Father, they teach us so much more about holiness and playfulness. They have open hearts and we sit there like stuffed shirts. I'm going for a nice walk!" '

'Margaret, you have a national overview, how do you see things at the present time?'

'Well, I rejoice at what's happening as this will help with the evangelism of children. It's growing gradually, not exploding as some feared, which has to mean that parishes are engaging with this seriously, and it's an area with much more depth than simply what we do for children. People are saying that their parishes have been transformed by engaging with this process. I remember a young priest at a recent Synod coming up to the microphone and saying, "I was against this but I am a convert and it has enriched and reinvigorated our life in Christ." As adults we need to be prepared to lose a degree of control and let the children come, for then they will lead us into new and exciting places.'

5

Hands on – hands open to receive

Implementing change in parish and cathedral

For those who are considering looking at the whole area of the admission of baptized children to Holy Communion in your church, there is help available. There will be parishes in your deanery or diocese who will have experience of this practice and they will be glad to be asked to tell you their story. Do not think that you will be able to transport their methods to your situation, or that the results will be the same for your community. Each parish is unique and needs to engage with this process of change in a way and at a pace that is right for the people there who gather regularly around the Lord's Table. There will be diocesan officers and committee members who will be able to help, and perhaps come along to make a presentation.

Your Diocesan Children's Adviser should be an early point of contact. These experts will have wide experience; they will be aware of what has happened elsewhere, and know the process of permission specific to your diocese. They are by nature enthusiastic people who will help you to gain confidence.

Likewise, the members of the Diocesan Liturgical Committee will be able to advise, especially on practical matters and all-age worship principles. Any exploration of children in church demands an understanding of All Age Worship. There really is more than enough readily available help out there, no matter how uncertain you may feel. Similarly, no matter how certain you may be, remember that others will not be so certain, and it is equally important for you to gain the experience and advice of others.

Bearing in mind all the help that is out there, I offer here my personal experience gained from the places in which I have served. This is not the last word in good practice, but it is real. Working together as Eucharistic communities, we were hands on, yet sought to open our hands to receive what God was giving us to make us whole.

Branksome St Aldhelm

Branksome is a suburb of Poole in Dorset. It borders one of the richest and most beautiful parishes in the country, but our parish wasn't like that. We had the railway, the old gasworks and MFI. We were typical of most English urban parishes, born out of Victorian expansion. If I had to pick an ordinary, middle-of-the-road parish for this chapter that most readers would recognize, we were it. Of course, no parish is ever ordinary. I had the most wonderful people to serve with, a great church school and the best fish 'n' chip shop for miles. We also had the factory where all your holiday sticks of rock are made, the sweet aroma regularly wafting across to the Vicarage.

St Aldhelm's had seen better times. I went there in 1992 at the tender age of twenty-eight. There were sixty regular worshippers on a Sunday, twice that number on the rather dog-eared Electoral Roll. Parish Share (Quota in those days of course) was more than a year behind, the church hall was falling down, the organ falling apart and there were only twelve people in full-time employment in the congregation. By bringing our first child to church, we discovered that we doubled the number of children in the main service on the first Sunday (a statistic I use to cheer myself up with in darker moments). The people in the Parish Profile were asking for change and growth, although few knew what that meant or how to achieve such development. However, as in most Anglican parishes, there were a faithful few who believed that things could change and that they were prepared to sacrifice many things to ensure this became a reality.

At this stage I was not a convert to children and communion. I hadn't done the thinking and it wasn't a big issue. Two main things were to inform my thinking in the years ahead: All Age Worship and our celebration of Holy Baptism. To that extent I can honestly say that God led us to a new awareness and that we ended up in a place beyond any expectations.

Things did change; as I write this I'm on a train to Brighton to see one of those who came to faith and joined the congregation, bringing along his wife (who later was confirmed) and children (who later were baptized and admitted to communion). This evening, he will be licensed as a Team Vicar in his new parish. God is good.

All of us together

I suppose the first thing that happened in Branksome was preaching on the importance of Baptism: 'every member ministry' stuff, 'What difference does this make to our daily lives?', and 'What are you going to do about it?' kind of sermons. The liturgy was updated and celebrated with a degree of warmth and welcome. Firmer links were made with the school, where I became a visitor at least once a week. Above all else we started praying, whether there was anyone there or not. The church had to be locked during the day, but I opened it on three occasions every day at published times for the daily offices and a daily Eucharist. This was a leap of faith similar to the ones of starting a Sunday School and Youth Group with no members, but slowly we grew, in attendance at worship and the number of children. The best evangelism is done by word of mouth; people heard something was going on and they came for a look. There is a real need for church out there, people want to come; often what stops them is the way we do things.

Six months in, I took a paper to the PCC on All Age Worship and, in particular, Eucharistic All Age Worship for us on the first Sunday of the month. It wasn't very consultative but then this was new territory for them and we needed to change fast. I've never again had something change all at once and so quickly. Honeymoons may be short-lived but they're worth going on. A date was set, the uniformed organizations were encouraged to attend and each child at the school received a personal invitation. An order of service, specific to the occasion, was prepared. People came. The congregation more than doubled. The main changes to the service were somewhat obvious: length, positioning of liturgical furniture, use of a radio-microphone, children and adults leading readings and prayers, carefully chosen music, post-service refreshments.

Short-term success is not hard to achieve but, as the months and years went on, this became an established part of our pattern and picked up the typical 'first Sunday of the month' label. It is important that we were aware from the outset that this is a pattern that is organic, constantly changing, and that just because something works well once, equal amounts of time and preparation need to go in each time to keep things fresh. It is a liturgical premise that the easiest service to do is something like a traditional High Mass. Everything is ordered, everyone has their assigned task and the liturgy is similar in almost all respects to the time before. Much more challenging is the act of All Age Worship which is based around a structure and can change completely in character each time it is prepared. Both are equally valid and have their place.

People and problems

Success flushes out opposition. As the service bedded down, more families joined the weekly congregation and in profile we became considerably younger. The Parish Profile had been asking for this change and so had everybody else, to survive as a parish if nothing else, but when you get what you ask for, it can come as a bit of a shock. Issues about noise and sitting still became pretty regular. Leadership becomes very important here; the Vicar has to be seen to be welcoming to those who are young and old and sometimes this means managing change and expectation. We live in an adult church and children need advocacy. Jesus had to do the same; it was the disciples who regularly got in their way.

Preaching became even more important, taking opportunities from the lectionary to teach about what being the whole people of God really means. Adults have a weapon of mass destruction in church far more powerful than any screaming child. The withering look to the new, nervous Christian with teething child in tow can put enquirers off church for life. I remember once it was Remembrance Sunday. Remembrance was an important day for Branksome; the parish had been bombed and the War Memorial was inside the church, and we inherited the tradition of reading out the names of the fallen from both wars, just before the silence at 11 a.m., towards the end of the Parish Eucharist. The congregation had grown like Topsy and it became clear that the children really ought to stay in for this important act. With solemn dignity we processed to the War Memorial, with veterans from World War II carrying the poppy wreath. The Last Post was sounded, the silence began, the silence continued, a child squealed and then screamed at the top of its voice, the mother whisked the child out of the building as fast as possible, the silence ended and the bugler sounded the Reveille. After the service, I had a queue of disgusted adults complaining to me about the noisy child. One last old lady came to speak to me, my heart sinking from the thought of more criticism. She told me to take no notice; it was wonderful the children were there. I had read her husband's name out from the War Memorial. How he would have liked to hear the cry of that child. How many children would have loved the chance of life to be able to squeal. Remembrance, she said, was not just about the past but also about the future – future peace. That is why her husband died, that others might live in peace, like the noisy child.

Concerns about the conduct of children may sometimes be reasonable, but they are not always correct. It is important to be able to distinguish between the constructive contribution and critical prejudice. There is a balance to be found between toddler anarchy and adult reserve. It is important that we understand what it is like to bring small children to church and that God's house is an environment where they can flourish. Running around shouting without parental control is clearly unacceptable but we must always remember that children are children and not mini adults. Children don't walk, they run, it's natural to them; adults lose the need and the puff. Clear advice should be given to parents about how to worship in the company of others, but not before a welcome is both offered and a reality. Welcoming a family and then telling them what they can't do is no welcome at all.

We introduced a quiet corner with toys and books and colouring. Occasionally a purge was required in the toy box as weapons of war or battery operated things that go bleep during the intercessions seemed to have appeared out of nowhere. Adults do the same with mobile phones. Busy Bags can be provided and children acknowledged properly in each act of worship, even if they are about to leave for Sunday School or equivalent.

A crèche can become, as it did in Branksome, a vital refuge for parents with small children to retreat to during quieter parts of the service. Here children can express themselves and feel safe and parents can talk to each other and discover solidarity. In my experience a crèche is a seed ground for growing new disciples and is as much for the benefit of the adults as it is for the children.

In church, adults who moan about children need often to examine their own behaviour, chatting in the queue for communion or after receiving communion. I often had to challenge complainers that they were behaving no differently than the children and they should know better. It is good over time to have a number of lay leaders, especially churchwardens, on board with an understanding of how to deal with those who complain about the inclusion of children. The priest cannot do everything or see everything; real welcoming has to be a team effort. It needs to be remembered that adults can complain about children, children cannot complain about adults – they just don't come again. Dealing with these issues is a constant struggle and never fully goes away.

Comparisons between 'how it was in my day' and now are false. Looking back in the registers for the century since the church was opened, either children were not recorded for their attendance or they hardly came. And now, the majority who did come came with only one parent, and half had only one parent to come with them anyway. Families, in whatever shape or size, must feel that they have a friend in the leadership of a church and can discuss their concerns openly. Such support needs to come personally and from the pulpit. All Age Worship must mean that, though; it's not just about children and every effort must be made to ensure that all, who have equal status before the Lord, have equal access to him through worship.

Real equality?

It soon became clear as numbers grew that we were not practising what we were preaching. We had become an all-age community in every way other than in the most important or most defining characteristic. I looked into the scriptural and traditional aspects of children receiving communion and soon realized that this had been missing from my training and professional understanding. When the penny dropped, I could not quite believe just how obvious this was and how rule-driven the Church was. Discrimination was alive and well in the Church and in my parish and at the altar!

If baptism was the great sacrament of being in Christ and of belonging to the church, and if this was the basis of our renewal, how could the daily and weekly outward and visible sign of that belonging be denied to some simply because of their age? I tested this thinking out on my diocesan bishop who was clearly on board and who gave great encouragement and teaching to me. Others in the diocese were moving at the same pace and we rapidly built a small network of support and enthusiasm.

The question was how to introduce this to the church. After sharing the vision with churchwardens and children's leaders it seemed right to do the same as before, and lead from the front by preaching about the whole subject. The people were used to the 'baptism is important' approach but this time I went further and described the rationale behind children and communion. For many, the realization on their faces was clear even from the distance of the pulpit; for others it was 'a nice idea vicar but it doesn't apply to us' response, and others were just quiet.

The next step was to take the subject to the PCC. We often worked in study mode, taking time out from the regular agenda to look at mission areas or to receive teaching so that members were informed about their faith as well as responsible for drains and gutters. The Diocesan Children's Adviser visited and we came up with a plan of development. Ours was a parish which took the Blessed Sacrament seriously and so concern for reverence and administration was keenly felt. If only I had known to what extent.

Wendy's story

Wendy was our PCC Secretary. She sang in the choir. She was married to the churchwarden who was involved in my appointment to the parish. She was a friend, the ideal PCC Secretary, quiet, supportive and affirming. Wendy was certainly the most prayerful member of the PCC and probably also of the congregation. Over a period of time discussions continued, and Wendy kept quiet. The debate in meetings and in the congregation was being won, even though we would be the first parish in the diocese to make this move. My enthusiasm and bravado grew as I became the co-ordinator of a group in the diocese to promote children and communion in the parishes. All seemed to be going well. There were some opponents but they were the usual suspects who by now I'd become used to working with. Then, as we made the decision in PCC, I could feel Wendy becoming more and more uncomfortable. Still she said nothing. Finally, after the meeting, I asked her what the problem was, and she then proceeded to tell me of her deep misgivings and painful agonizing that had been going on inside her all through this process. I was stunned – she had made no fuss and was certainly one of the brightest and most sensitive among our number. For Wendy not to be on board with this was bad enough, for her to be tortured by it was almost worth packing the whole thing in as a bad idea. We met and talked it over a couple of times.

Wendy loved children, had children of her own, but valued the sacrament so highly that this just felt wrong. There were too many ragged edges for her. For Wendy, this was a spiritual issue, forcing her to examine how she reacted to changes and, in particular, how she felt about God and the church that was doing this to her. After a fortnight of soul searching, and absenting herself from communion, Wendy was there at the regular Thursday Eucharist. With the curate due to preside, I chose to sit next to her. In solitary prayer together the service continued. At the time for communion I stood to let her out of the pew but Wendy preferred to stay in her place. I decided that I needed to stand alongside this member of the congregation just as much as the children. All ages and all stages. Without receiving communion I sat back down. If Wendy felt that strongly, but with such humility, the least I could do was to be where she was, if only for a moment. The service ended and we chatted briefly. A few days later we admitted children to communion for the first time. Wendy was there. The combination of her prayers, my refraining from the sacrament to be with her in her lonely place, and her love conquering all had broken through her opposition. She had decided that sharing communion with baptized children said more about the love of God than withholding it until such times as they passed tests set by the church. Eventually things came full circle, and Wendy agreed to speak about her feelings at a major diocesan conference on the subject, describing her painful but holy journey. Wendy tells her own story in Appendix 3.

The first Sunday

We did a substantial course of preparation for the children due to receive communion, culminating in a workshop day when they made me a chasuble to wear on the first Sunday, decorated with little pictures of their faces. I looked a twit but they felt, for the first time, that they knew what the funny clothes were about and that they were part of this celebration.

As we were the first parish in the diocese to undertake this new policy, the Bishop came to preside at the Parish Eucharist and to admit the children. The Bishop had taken no persuasion that the diocesan guidelines should have no set age threshold, so on that day seventy children of all ages came to stand before him. His face shone as he enjoyed their enthusiasm and their seriousness as he placed the host in their hands. There were no problems at the rail. Both during the service and on subsequent Sundays, it was as if things had always been done like this. It felt normal and the church felt younger and more complete.

There were unexpected events though. First, a number of silent but sceptical folk came forward to offer their support after seeing that all was well, and that the administration of communion had not fallen apart. Then we all noticed how the children, even when there were large numbers present, had become quieter in the service, especially at the Eucharistic Prayer, because now it included them and was not some long monologue by some bloke at the front towards the end of the service when they were getting fed up. In fact, instead of getting fed up, they realized they were being fed. Interest grew in what was going on up at the altar, and this in a church where the altar was a long way off, behind a big rood screen. Adult confirmation candidates often speak of missing the personal blessing received at the distribution of communion, but children don't see it in this way. They see others receiving something special and they can't work out why it's not for them. Most unexpectedly, three people, three parents in fact, came forward over a period of time to make a personal confession. The fact that their children had been through a course of teaching and learning (we need to get away from the word 'instruction') had prompted them to consider their own commitment. For two of them this meant offering themselves for confirmation and one for baptism and confirmation. All three had been receiving communion for years, because 'that's what everybody else did'. Children and Communion provides a mission opportunity for the whole church, not just children. It is about nurture, which should be a constant activity of the church and for all, whatever stage of understanding and belonging each person has reached.

Good news spreads fast

Soon the telephone was ringing. Interested parishes wanted to know how it had gone and how things had settled down. A new team was set up under one of the diocesan boards and together we prepared a substantial booklet that went to all parishes in the diocese with an encouraging letter from the bishop. Members of the team were increasingly asked to visit parishes to talk about the subject and to encourage development. In February 1998 a major residential diocesan conference was organized for those expressing an interest in admitting children. It was entitled 'Children and Communion – Food for Thought', and over eighty people attended. It opened with worship, and all participants were invited to recall their baptismal vows. The Bishop led the opening session and other speakers included a Diocesan Children's Adviser (from another diocese), the Diocesan Continuing Ministerial Education Officer and a parish priest from Ealing who told the conference about real experience in an 'experimental' parish. He spoke about their way of tackling the subject – the four P's: Principle, Procedure, Preparation and Pitfalls. Wendy and other lay people including children's leaders described their own insights.

The view of the conference was overwhelmingly positive although some were still concerned about how much children might 'understand' what it was they were receiving. I think this is the bottom line for many adults. It is in this area that the greatest change of thinking is required in seeing the receiving of Holy Communion more as food for the journey of faith, and for all, than as a sign of complete commitment and comprehension. This is only part of a wider understanding of the Church as a moving, organic, living and changing body rather than as a mature but more static repository of belief and witness. The pilgrim people are travelling; therefore, by definition, their perspective will change. Adults have to ask themselves how much they 'understand' and whether they are setting false standards for children in comparison to themselves. We do not need to pass a GCSE in Eucharistic theology in order to receive communion but we do need to be part of the life-long learning process of the church. Receiving Christ in the sacrament is not just a cerebral experience but involves our whole being. Surely children have more chance of comprehending the sacrament if they are part of the meal in a meaningful and valuable way. Families eat together, and the children are often served first not last.

The church has a vocation to embody the equality of the love of Christ in all aspects of human life, and adults in the church need to 'understand' that this applies to children in equal terms. We do not quiz people at the altar rail who come to church once a year at the Midnight Mass about whether they are confirmed or to what degree they understand what they are doing. An invitation is issued, clarification is given if needed, and the people come forward. And yet, we are prepared to withhold communion from those who are often most eager to learn, most enthusiastic to belong. Any church considering introducing the admission of baptized children to communion before confirmation really ought to consider a parallel course for the whole congregation to discover and rediscover the meaning and depth of receiving Christ himself in the form of bread and wine.

Unexpected place

When you introduce children to communion, unexpected things happen. First, as we found immediately, the children took to it with increased commitment and so did parents, who described a change of mood at home. Praying at home, as a family, seemed to be more acceptable and desirable, for the relationship between parent and child had changed. Status is important for humans and having equal status before God is part of the liberation brought in by God's Kingdom. Grace before meals became less embarrassing and invitations arrived on the Vicarage doorstep for me to visit and celebrate a Eucharist at the home of a number of families. Adults came forward asking to discover more about their faith and a whole new culture of learning, especially through Emmaus courses, became easy to encourage. As the church became younger, so we became more enthusiastic to learn.

However, the greatest change led us to a most unexpected place. Everything was going well, but after a year or so we were growing increasingly uncomfortable. Everything was in place, the preparation course and on-going nurture in Sunday School, but something seemed to be missing. Like many churches, we celebrated Holy Baptism on Sunday mornings during the main service. There were about fifty baptisms a year, too many to do every week, so they were clustered into groups of four to six and the Parish Eucharist adapted accordingly. But with our great emphasis on the importance of baptism, it seemed increasingly incongruous to be admitting people to the faith, and then carrying on to celebrate a major sign of that faith and withhold it from them. This applied not just to infants but to whole families who, while perhaps not committed, were certainly moved by what we were doing with them. Including people in something special is a much better mission practice than leading people (quite literally) to water and then not letting them drink. This, we agreed in PCC, was a much more Eastern Orthodox approach which appealed to us but was not realistic in real circumstances. Maybe it would be in many years' time when generations of children had been receiving communion for years, but not now.

So after much deliberation we decided to try one Sunday where the main service was a non-Eucharistic baptism service and we moved the Parish Eucharist to Sunday evening. Branksome is a solidly Eucharistic parish so this was either brave or reckless. A great deal of communication was given and much work put into the liturgy of both services. Some people were clearly unhappy. Some on the other hand were pleased, especially those who had to work on a Sunday and those who valued a quieter, more reflective, celebration than the hustle and bustle of the morning numbers. Instead of font and altar, font and paschal candle became the important furniture in church and so we turned all four hundred chairs round to face each other, cantoris and decani style, so that we could model the journey motif by leading the service from one focal point to the other. Teaching was given to welcome people to Holy Baptism, and to teach them about how they would grow into the Eucharistic community. Candidates came to a normal Sunday before their date and after the baptism day. Welcomers, whom they had met before, sat with them in church. The focus was on our guests and what God was doing for them.

Baptism was important enough to stand alone and to be rediscovered by the regular congregation. The words of the Welcome really meant something, because that was why we were there.

There is one Lord, one faith, one baptism:
N and N, by one Spirit we are all baptized into one body.
We welcome you into the fellowship of faith;
we are children of the same heavenly Father;
we welcome you.

To be honest, some regular members of the congregation chose not to come. The thought of not receiving communion on Sunday morning was too much for them, and not without good reason. We arranged lifts to bring less mobile folk to church in the evening when it was dark in the winter. People enjoyed the evening service as it had a different character and we could do things with music and darkness and light, but for some time on it felt strange. However, this Baptism Sunday, as it became called, was proving to be a mission-shaped opportunity and families went away really feeling as if they had joined something and with a strong sense that God had touched them while they were surrounded by the church which had gathered for that purpose alone. With our explanations, they knew that the next step was to grow in faith and commitment soon, as they would then be welcomed at the meal shared at all other times. We felt we couldn't offer communion to our own number, those who were 'in', quite literally in the face of those who were coming forward, for whatever reason and whatever commitment, without going against all that we had come to stand for as a church. Clearly this was a hybrid solution and not suitable for many places, but it seemed to complete our journey where all are admitted by virtue of their baptism and communion and everything else flows from that essential fact. It must have something to it, as the service continues to thrive seven years on.

The Cathedral and Abbey Church of St Alban

I never wanted to work in a cathedral. As someone rooted in and fulfilled by the parochial ministry, I had always thought that was where I would be for many years. But God had other plans and so we moved to an unfamiliar place and an unfamiliar role. St Albans is probably the most 'parish' of all the parish church cathedrals. The congregations are large and regular and there has been a long tradition of families and good children's work. However, in such places it is easy to take things for granted and good attendance is not always a test of effectiveness. Part of the brief on arriving was to come to a decision on whether or not to introduce children and communion. The Abbey community had been discussing the issue for four years or more but there had always seemed to be something to distract from implementation. This was reflected in the diocese, where good work by way of preparation had been done but there was no clear drive to push this forward. The diocese had a minimum age set at seven and, while this was put in place for well-argued reasons, as others had found, such a set age acts as a disincentive.

It seemed to me that the best way to break the logjam was to use the same approach as at Branksome over All Age Worship – pick the subject you want to use up in your 'honeymoon' period and go for it. Within eight months the decision had been made, and in addition All Age Worship, similar to last time but fresher, was introduced each month. The people here are intellectual, informed and cosmopolitan and many parents were pushing for this development. Introducing communion for baptized children was my first big project, and although it went through smoothly it still seemed to be like turning a supertanker in terms of keeping this 'big ship' on course. The preparation course took place but I was beginning to feel that, with these sessions, less is more. Cathedrals struggle with encouraging a sense of belonging, and enabling people to feel that a church is theirs is a constant challenge in a complex, multi-layered organization.

Clarity is a virtue, as is good communication, consultation and collaboration. A large number of children were admitted on the first Sunday, and once again, afterwards, it seemed that it had always been so. The sense of this was conspicuous on the following Sunday as everything seemed normal – 'as it was, is now and ever shall be'. In time we discovered that the best way for us to do preparation was through a special class each year in Sunday Club time through the weeks of Lent. As well as ensuring that nurture about communion was on-going, we found it helpful to be focused in this way, the children receiving communion for the first time at Easter.

There is one other thing I ought to recount about St Albans. We are blessed with a beautiful and historic building but, if you are little, it is just about as difficult to use as it can possibly be. Let me explain: at Branksome, when the children returned for communion from their activities in Sunday School and crèche in the church hall, they were able to come in the back of the church and take their places discreetly at just the right time. In St Albans the opposite is true. The only space we have for teaching and nurture is in the Chapter House, which is some considerable distance from the nave of the Abbey. In coming back to the service, the children have to be called at just the right time in order to stop what they are doing, clear up, exchange the Peace and then start the return journey. This means leaving the crypt under the Chapter House and negotiating a corridor one person wide, with two fire doors and two flights of steps. Then there is another staircase, a narrow Norman doorway, and then what seems like a quarter of a mile of transept and ambulatory. There are distracting things along the way also, such as toilets and a colourful bookstall. Getting often around 150 children and helpers through this obstacle course is a logistical nightmare. Then children have to gather together to arrive en bloc as they can only enter the nave stage-front, in full view of the congregation with their mixture of adoring/understanding/annoyed/bored/surprised faces.

In reality, apart from this being a weekly challenge, something powerful happens. In the nave of the Abbey we can hear the children coming; their volume increases despite the best efforts of parents and helpers until there is this burst of energy upon the congregation just as the Eucharist is coming to a crescendo. Three Sundays a month the children return for the Great Amen (the other Sunday we are all in together throughout the whole service), and there is this powerful yet slightly chaotic rush of what feels like the Holy Spirit that is impossible to ignore as the doors are opened and the children come in. The adults have had their nurture; the children have had theirs; and, together once more, we settle down to pray together with the words that include 'give us this day our daily bread'. It's not ideal but it's necessary and yet it teaches us all something as we live with the realities of our building that reflect the realities of life. We wouldn't design it like this but this is how we are and we come together again to find our place around the holy table.

Take, Bless, Break, Share

There are many preparation courses (which will be reviewed later) available to the Church. At the Abbey we soon decided that, if good nurture was to be on-going and part of our regular pattern, courses for communion preparation should be concise, focused and easily updated each year. The five Sundays of Lent seemed to be a natural time for this to take place. We decided to follow the *Common Worship* model of agreeing a structure for any such course, which different leaders and resources could then adapt to the needs of the children each year. Every service of *Common Worship* has a structure printed before the liturgical resources themselves. This structure includes the vital components for each service. Onto this framework other resources can be added to suit the day and season. Using this approach, the vital components of a preparation course for children can be kept fresh with new and interesting material from a wide range of resources.

At St Albans, we have used this approach now for two years and it has proved very successful. The first 'given' is that this course is recognized as only part of the full Sunday Club curriculum and that teaching and nurture in this area take place all year and are part of the regular subject matter for a church where children receive communion. Sunday Club leaders are signed up to this and re-inforce the concept year round. The congregation know that the course comes round at the same time of year and, while they are in Lent Groups and other devotional studies, the children are focusing in the same way. Easter is a natural time to admit the children and Corpus Christi and/or Pentecost are useful times for a follow-up session or party. The course has been given the name Communion Club, which seems to say what it is and what it does in relation to Sunday Club (our name for Sunday School). Each week of the course there is a title, which represents part of the Eucharistic action, and a scriptural text to reflect upon. Then core or structure headings are used for the leaders to plan their resources around. Worksheets are produced so that a small file can be put together, to include lots of other relevant information about church (e.g. children are asked to search out the parish magazine and other material). During the course each family receives a home visit and on completion each child is given a certificate of communicant status. Communion Club is lay led with a priest coming along one week to join in the fun and to teach about the practicalities of receiving communion. Another advantage of this approach is that it can be adapted to different ages and used at other times, not just at first preparation.

Take

This is largely about discovering and recording biographical information about the child and the church. Jesus 'takes' us and calls us by name into life with him through Holy Baptism.

'I have called you by name, you are mine.' (Isaiah 43.1)

- Children are helped to complete a sheet which asks for the child's name, age, address, telephone number, e-mail address, date of birth, date and place of baptism (looking in church registers for your own name can be fun).
- A welcome is given with words from the baptism service and an awareness of membership of the church described through action and pictures.
- The Liturgy of the Word in a Eucharist is described, there being a space on the sheet to put this week's readings.
- Learn how to look up a Bible reference.
- A commitment is made by the child to try to read the Bible regularly (a signature is asked for – kids love this) and to ask for help at home about how to do this best.
- Collect information about the local church to which you belong: Sunday notice sheet, parish magazine, leaflets and so on.
- Pictures and colour should be used on any printed material.

Bless

This session looks at the ways in which Jesus blesses us, especially through the Sacraments.

'Jesus said to them, "I am the bread of life. Whoever comes to me will never be hungry, and whoever believes in me will never be thirsty."' (John 6.35)

- Children think of three ways in which God has blessed them, either over all their life or just recently, and fill in their new sheet.
- We discover the seven Sacraments by using a simple card game of symbols and descriptions (a bit like 'pairs') and write down what is discovered.

- We learn the definition of a sacrament off by heart: 'A sacrament is an outward and visible sign of an inward and spiritual grace.'
- We think of how Jesus shares himself with us through the sacraments and the children go home to test their parents, to see if they can think of all seven sacraments and their signs and meaning.

Break

This session is more hands-on. The children look at the Passion and try to make the link between the death of Jesus and his resurrection.

'Then he took a loaf of bread, and when he had given thanks, he broke it and gave it to them, saying, "This is my body, which is given for you. Do this in remembrance of me."' (Luke 22.19)

- The Triduum (the three days of Maundy Thursday, Good Friday and Holy Saturday) is acted out with washing of feet, the Last Supper, Good Friday and Easter Day.
- Children are introduced to the bread and wine used in church and taught how to receive.
- Jesus' body was broken, the bread is broken: what did he say about the bread?
- This simple prayer of preparation is learnt and written out:

> With this bread that we bring
> **we shall remember Jesus.**
>
> With this wine that we bring
> **we shall remember Jesus.**
>
> Bread for his body,
> wine for his blood,
> gifts from God to his table we bring.
> **We shall remember Jesus.**

Share

This session works through Eucharistic Prayer H and a picture of the Last Supper is provided.

'When he was at the table with them, he took bread, blessed and broke it, and gave it to them. Then their eyes were opened and they recognized him.' (Luke 24.30–31a)

- On the sheet, write a letter to Jesus to thank him for what he is doing in the service of Holy Communion.
- These letters can be valued at a later date by being placed on the altar on the day of admission.

It must be remembered that this is a bare structure and not a stand-alone preparation course. The best preparation course of all has to be when all available resources are gathered and those involved in teaching prepare interesting and challenging material and presentations to suit the group of children concerned and the local circumstances, around an agreed structure. This structure is a way of delivering a concise but exciting course of discovery while encouraging understanding that can be owned and articulated by children. In preparation and participation, for adults and for children, the task is to engage, for that is what Christ is doing for us.

Practicalities and parents

Practical things about giving communion to children are important but no more important than in giving adults communion. In fact children react better to teaching and are generally less self-conscious than adults. Children display a unique spiritual awareness at the communion rail, and while on the odd occasion peer pressure can result in a little giggling this is no worse than the adult chatting that often takes place. Children learn by example. But also, children can give us an example. I well remember one Sunday in the parish when the Suffragan Bishop had come to celebrate and baptize on the Feast of the Baptism of Our Lord. Kris and Perry were brothers and they were to be baptized, aged six and eight. They were delightful tearaways, full of energy. The Bishop began the service in the normal way and everything was fine. He preached about the importance of understanding and living our baptismal faith. When it came to the time for baptism, standing at the large stone font placed centrally by the West door he called for those to be baptized to be presented. Kris and Perry leapt out of the front row, at the other end of the church, sprinted down the nave (I think Kris won), leapt up the steps beside the Bishop and threw their heads over the side of the font, waiting to be sploshed. The Bishop proclaimed, 'That is what I meant earlier; if we could all have that enthusiasm for our faith, the world would believe!' The congregation burst into applause. Children engage with special things differently from adults and we should not be surprised if it does not conform to our expectations.

So here are some practical points, born mostly out of experience rather than forethought.

- Parents, grandparents and members of the congregation – if you want children to wait quietly in line for communion, model this yourselves.
- Likewise, be a good example at the communion rail. Children will copy you.
- The person distributing the bread needs to know the congregation. If a minimum age for receiving communion has been set, you need to know those who will put their hands out to receive. This also helps spot visitors who may have been admitted elsewhere. While children will copy others, confident hands usually receive (it is the same for adults). If in doubt, do not be shy; you have control – ask the person if they normally receive Holy Communion.

- The person with the bread may need to indicate to the person administering the wine that a child is to receive. Think about how to do this naturally.
- If a child is small, too small for chalice to get between chin and rail, ask them to stand up. It's not rocket science.
- Children are more used to having a cup held for them than adults.
- Normal administration rules apply; if a wafer is dropped or something else goes wrong, just act accordingly.
- If communion is administered standing up (i.e., there is no communion rail in use) the adults may well need to bend knees to help the child (who can't get taller).
- Many parents wish to break their wafer to share with a very small child. If the child is baptized, let the parent be in control: God can cope.
- If a child does not like to receive the wine, that is OK; they will have received communion in full as per the church's tradition.
- If in doubt with any of the above, speak to the people at the communion rail. We have a habit of not speaking at this important moment in the liturgy, but actually this says more about our reserve than about the solemnity of the moment.
- Finally, a word about blessings at the communion rail, which do not really fall within my remit but are important acts of love and devotion. When we bless children, we should bend down or, better, bend our knees to be face to face. They find it easier and it is less dismissive. Children will often bring toys to be blessed. As a general rule, bless them too (and guide dogs too), for all we are doing is modelling God's love for all, rather than engaging in some deep exercise with ontological significance. My previous boss here at the Abbey used to draw a theological line at blessing plastic weapons of mass destruction, but we could never find one so it never became an issue. Communion and blessing are

about the pouring out of God's love and we are sharing in that amazing generosity. We must not be anything less than generous ourselves.

Parents are key to all of this, as key as the Church itself. The Church must take seriously its partnership with parents in the area of children and communion. Some families will be enthusiastic. Some will want to wait, and that position must be fully respected and upheld by the leadership of the church as a completely acceptable and honourable status. No-one must be made to feel left out by this process within a church community. So long as that is made abundantly clear, those families who choose to continue with the inherited pattern of the church seem to be able to do so with complete integrity.

Visit families at home. Celebrate the Eucharist with them. Talk to them. Teach the parents as well as the children. Learn from both. This is mission in action and we must be hands-on for then we will receive the love of God in the form of bread and wine – all of us.

6

The children come

The Church welcomes children to communion

At Easter, the Confirmation Service with the biggest numbers for many years took place at St Albans Cathedral. This is the first year that those admitted to Holy Communion had been eligible for Confirmation. They have been retained and have come forward to learn and discover more with unrivalled enthusiasm. It works.

After many years of discussion and discernment, the whole Church came to value this sharing of the gifts of God in a new way in early 2006.

The debate in the February 2006 General Synod

The debate was sincere and open. Calls were made for research in the future and for an emphasis on nurture. This is an important point, because nurture is something for the whole Church, constantly, and not just for those at the beginning of their Christian journey. I tried to answer this and other commonly asked questions in a speech called early on:

> At long last this Synod has today a chance to legislate for something that Christ himself has encouraged us to do, to 'let the children come', and for Synod to do this with perhaps some child-like qualities required for inclusion in the Kingdom of God, openness, innocence and enthusiasm.
>
> Now there are some commonly asked questions in this area which perhaps need looking at again.

Does this change our inherited pattern of baptism, confirmation and communion? Well, no, as we've heard and because this process is gradual and developmental. It will be all right as this grows. This is evolution not revolution.

What about teaching and preparation? Well, we do need rigour, as the previous speaker has said, but the rigour should be in our nurture and teaching for all ages, not just for the children. We can't single them out as a special needs group, we all have those special needs. We should be learning throughout our Christian journey.

What about confirmation? Well, confirmation is not under threat. This is anecdotal, but in the place in which I work (St Albans Abbey), those who have been admitted to communion at their earliest possible age have come forward this year for confirmation. It's the first time we've seen them come through in our particular place. So this year, we have the largest confirmation of young people that anybody can remember. Perhaps it does actually work!

And what about this question of how much children can believe or confess? Well, if on-going nurture is in place as it should be for all ages, all of the time, children can know and celebrate the Eucharist with us and bring something unique in terms of their understanding of it and their articulation of it as awe and wonder, perhaps some of those gifts that we adults often forget. We sang about this yesterday in our hymn:

> Here our children find a welcome,
> in the shepherd's flock and fold,
> here as bread and wine are taken
> Christ sustains us as of old.

I didn't choose the hymn but it seemed appropriate.

I believe we should vote this legislation through with as much unanimity as possible. It's not something we get to do that often. The admission of all baptized persons to communion is, classically, a Fresh Expression: something faithful to scripture and tradition and yet a new expression of this living tradition. The Orthodox Church has known this all down the ages.

So let's have confidence in our children. So let's have confidence in our teachers, let's have confidence in our parishes to get this right. And let's have confidence in the gifts God will give us by welcoming children. Jesus was clear as this Synod should be clear, 'Let the children come.'

The speech was welcomed but the most telling words came from one of the youngest members of the Synod, Simon Butterworth, who is one of the youth representatives. He told of his work among children and young people and invited anyone who doubted their spirituality or ability to understand they were welcome to come and join his year group who would convince them once and for all. But when he pointed out that children have to provide certificates and do special classes, saying: 'I'm concerned that we are now asking more of our children than we are of adults in our churches,' this drew warm applause.

The Bishop of Durham (the Rt Revd Tom Wright) concluded the speeches from the floor by pointing out that in the time that the Church had been discussing the move, he had become both a father and now a grandfather. With his usual theological clarity he reminded the Synod that this was really an argument about baptism, and whether it was a full initiation, and whether the Eucharist was food for the journey. He said, 'Most of us believe it is both.'

The regulations were given final approval by a show of hands with a substantial majority.

After so long in discussion and after so much effort by many to welcome children to communion, that is how it all ended in February 2006 – the Synod voted to move to the next business. The headline in the *Church Times* read: 'Space cleared at altar rail for children'.

Now we've made it

So children are now welcomed on equal terms at the Eucharist in the Church of England. There is still much to do, a lot of growing up needs to happen. Parishes up and down the country need to engage with this legislation. Even if a parish has few or no children among its regular number, all have to be ready for when children present themselves in church. Not to be ready and to therefore refuse a communicant child would be a complete failure of pastoral ministry, if not worse. We all need to do some work.

- Clergy must be ready and informed. Deanery Chapters need to have this subject on their agenda as soon as possible. Continuing Ministerial Education officers need to consider regular in-service training for clergy to equip those with little experience.
- Archdeacons should include among their Articles of Enquiry questions about preparation, participation and progress. PCCs need to put this on the agenda and take advice. Nurture programmes need preparing and revising.
- Bishops need to revise their diocesan guidelines in accordance with the new regulations and continue to support those who promote work among children in their diocese.
- Diocesan Children's Advisers need to tell the dioceses that this change has finally come and be ready, perhaps with teams of people, to support those engaged in change.

Age restrictions

Some dioceses still have age restrictions in their diocesan guidelines. Now would be an opportune time to revisit this hurdle which is not represented in the national regulations. Several dioceses have no age restrictions and they have not found this to cause any problems. Parishes are well able to develop their own practice in this area and are probably best placed to know what is right in their situation. I have had to work both systems: no age limit in one diocese, and a minimum age of seven in another. There is a greater responsibility placed on priest and parents to get this right if there is no arbitrary restriction. Families can work this out for themselves and will do so effectively. If there is an arbitrary age restriction it only serves to exclude some who are ready to receive Holy Communion and to impose yet another false distinction.

No-one would advocate indiscriminate distribution of the sacrament but the emphasis here must be on baptismal status and food for the journey. There will inevitably be a mixed economy but congregations are well used to living with such matters. In our current confirmation group for young people there are those who have been previously admitted to communion and those who have chosen to wait. They don't have a problem with understanding this. We achieve more by inclusion and freedom than by exclusion and restriction. Let's face it, age restrictions are not really there for the children, they are there to make the adults feel comfortable. Discernment is vital but it is not served by an arbitrary age. Good nurture and teaching should be the only requirement.

Nurture for all

Clearly, then, the most important matter for all is nurture. In Appendix 2 to this book resources and background reading are reviewed. But the best resource of all is active engagement with the issues and a total commitment for all ages to be constantly learning, developing and maturing their faith. One of the benefits found by many parishes is that participating in preparing children to receive communion changes the mindset, and nurture is promoted for all in whatever way is most appropriate. Parents want to learn more and seek out Alpha and Emmaus type courses. In those places which admit children, adult confirmation numbers rise because adults realize they too need more. It may well be that the children will be changing our church culture once and for all. Parishes should regularly review their total pattern of nurture and promote this as, literally, daily bread for the Christian.

Worship

By definition, the admission of children to Holy Communion before confirmation changes their place within the worship of the church. Therefore, the worship of the church will need to take into account their new place around the table. Parishes are having to review their Eucharistic worship in the light of these new regulations, not only practical details regarding the administration of communion but, more importantly, the inclusion of all ages in a meaningful way. The All Age Worship movement in the Church of recent years has always influenced Word Services or so-called Family Services but now this must be the case also for Eucharistic services. This will be the case not just for special or monthly services but for the regular Sunday pattern week by week. Many have had good experiences with regular all-age Eucharistic worship, especially using the style of preaching that can speak to children and adults on different levels at the same time. Such services do not need to have low common denominators.

At St Albans Cathedral, the second Sunday of the month sees the children in church throughout the service with preaching geared towards them, but with a powerful underlying message for adults included. The Parish Eucharist is celebrated with hundreds of people, organ, orchestral music group and authentic leadership by children and young people, and all within the hour. There is a special but regular order of service which includes Eucharistic Prayer H, a powerful tool that speaks to young and old alike. It would be easy to skip over this text, but read it to yourself now assuming your church admits children to communion and that you are one of those children, and feel the power of this prayer.

PRAYER H

The Lord be with you   or   The Lord is here.
and also with you.   **His Spirit is with us.**

Lift up your hearts.
We lift them to the Lord.

Let us give thanks to the Lord our God.
It is right to give thanks and praise.

It is right to praise you, Father, Lord of all creation;
in your love you made us for yourself.

When we turned away
you did not reject us,
but came to meet us in your Son.
**You embraced us as your children
and welcomed us to sit and eat with you.**

In Christ you shared our life
that we might live in him and he in us.
**He opened his arms of love upon the cross
and made for all the perfect sacrifice for sin.**

On the night he was betrayed,
at supper with his friends
he took bread, and gave you thanks;
he broke it and gave it to them, saying:
Take, eat; this is my body which is given for you;
do this in remembrance of me.

**Father, we do this in remembrance of him:
his body is the bread of life.**

At the end of supper, taking the cup of wine,
he gave you thanks, and said:
Drink this, all of you; this is my blood of the new covenant,
which is shed for you for the forgiveness of sins;
do this in remembrance of me.

**Father, we do this in remembrance of him:
his blood is shed for all.**

As we proclaim his death and celebrate his rising in glory,
send your Holy Spirit that this bread and this wine
may be to us the body and blood of your dear Son.

As we eat and drink these holy gifts
make us one in Christ, our risen Lord.

With your whole Church throughout the world
we offer you this sacrifice of praise
and lift our voice to join the eternal song of heaven:

Holy, holy, holy Lord,
God of power and might,
Heaven and earth are full of your glory.
Hosanna in the highest.

The service continues with the Lord's Prayer.

We've been using this prayer regularly at the Cathedral now for four years and it's noticeable how people are beginning to learn it off by heart. Despite this there is still a gaping hole in the Church's provision for children in terms of texts that can include them fully. Other denominations have cracked this one; so should the Church of England. The Liturgical Commission should now spend time preparing texts to meet children where they are by drawing not just on liturgical insights but also on the experience of those involved in education and learning. Children might just have something to say themselves about the subject as well.

A school Eucharist

It is not within my remit here to discuss the celebration of Holy Communion in schools. There are others better qualified to do this, but it is a developing area. However, it is also an area that needs really careful consultation, preparation and agreement. There is no point in holding a Eucharist in a school if it is going to re-inforce any sense of exclusion. The Diocesan Board of

Education ought to be a first port of call if you are considering such a move.

We did not celebrate a school Eucharist at Branksome. The context was not right to do so. We do celebrate a termly school Eucharist at St Albans, both for our own primary school and for the deanery comprehensive. They are two of the best services held regularly in the Abbey. For the Abbey Primary School, the service has full participation (and often planning) by the children, parents are welcome and admitted children receive communion while everyone else is welcome to receive an individual blessing. Each year, the year group of seven-year-olds are written to by the priest and invited to take part in the Communion Club preparation in church on Sundays during Lent. There is regular take-up and the communicant body of our church school is growing in numbers and commitment. The Townsend School Eucharist is a wonderful occasion when the nave is packed with students who celebrate the Eucharist with a reverence and concentration much better than many adult congregations. It takes time, but we also offer a blessing to all those who don't receive, which has a particular pleasure for the clergy since the popularity of hair gel has increased. In fact, at the time of writing, yesterday was Ash Wednesday and the school were in. Hundreds of young people received communion and most were blessed. Some beautiful modern songs were enjoyed by all, a sermon was preached, a drama was acted and the whole thing took exactly one hour. It is possible.

Conclusion

The legislation to admit baptized children to Holy Communion in the Church of England came into force on 15 June 2006 – the Feast of Corpus Christi, a day of thanksgiving for the Eucharist. In St Albans, by happy coincidence, this was the day that the children in Communion Club came together again to celebrate the Eucharist, reflect on their new experience and have a party. Most appropriate.

The intention of this book has been to tell the story of the admission of children to communion before confirmation in a way that parishes may find accessible and to provide an encouragement for the Church as a whole to seize this mission opportunity.

Children are mission-shaped. They are enthusiastic, open to change and growth; they contribute to others and bring their own spirituality and closeness to God. Children were welcomed by Jesus and bring an innocence we all need to enter the Kingdom. As the baptism and confirmation services say, they 'believe and trust'.

The admission of children to communion is a fresh expression of the response of the Church to the revelation in Jesus. We are more like him for including them. All parts of the Church, Catholic and Evangelical, can unite around this development and feel that their emphasis is respected and honoured.

Nurture is emphasized by including children and it should include us all, always.

Those places which have not considered this change in practice, for whatever reason, must now do so. It will help you grow. It will lead you to new opportunities and new pastoral relationships. Children and Communion will renew the life of your church, so go on, 'Let the children come . . .' to Communion.

This familiar prayer is best read as if from the mouths of the children, the children we have now welcomed to Holy Communion.

Father of all,
we give you thanks and praise,
that when we were still far off
you met us in your Son and brought us home.

Dying and living, he declared your love,
gave us grace, and opened the gate of glory.
May we who share Christ's body live his risen life;
we who drink his cup bring life to others;
we whom the Spirit lights give light to the world.
Keep us firm in the hope you have set before us,
so we and all your children shall be free,
and the whole earth live to praise your name;
through Christ our Lord.
Amen.

Appendix 1
General Synod (GS 1596A)

Admission of Baptised Children to Holy Communion Regulations 2006

The General Synod hereby makes the following Regulations under paragraph 1(c) of Canon B15A: –

1. These Regulations may be cited as the Admission of Baptised Children to Holy Communion Regulations 2006 and shall come into force on the fifteenth day of June 2006 as appointed by the Archbishops of Canterbury and York.
2. Children who have been baptised but who have not yet been confirmed and who are not yet ready and desirous to be confirmed as required by paragraph 1(a) of Canon B15A may be admitted to Holy Communion provided that the conditions set out in these Regulations are satisfied.
3. Every diocesan bishop may at any time make a direction to the effect that applications from parishes under these Regulations may be made in his diocese. The bishop's discretion in this respect shall be absolute, and he may at any time revoke such a direction (without prejudice to the validity of any permissions already granted thereunder).
4. Where a direction under paragraph 3 is in force in a diocese, an incumbent may apply to the bishop for permission that children falling within the definition in paragraph 2 may be admitted to Holy Communion in one or more of the parishes in the incumbent's charge. Such application must be made in writing and must be accompanied by a copy of a resolution in support of the application passed by the parochial church council of each parish in respect of which the application is made.
5. Before granting any permission under paragraph 4, the bishop must first satisfy himself (a) that the parish concerned has made adequate provision for preparation and continuing nurture in the Christian life and will encourage any child admitted to Holy Communion under

these Regulations to be confirmed at the appropriate time and (b) where the parish concerned is within the area of a local ecumenical project established under Canon B 44, that the other participating Churches have been consulted.

6. The bishop's decision in relation to any application under paragraph 4 shall be final, but a refusal shall not prevent a further application being made on behalf of the parish concerned, provided that at least one year has elapsed since the most recent previous application was refused.

7. Any permission granted under paragraph 4 shall remain in force unless and until revoked by the bishop. The bishop must revoke such permission upon receipt of an application for the purpose made by the incumbent. Such application must be made in writing and accompanied by a copy of a resolution in support of the application passed by the parochial church council of each parish in respect of which the application is made. Otherwise, the bishop may only revoke a permission granted under paragraph 4 if he considers that the conditions specified in paragraph 5 are no longer being satisfactorily discharged. Before revoking any permission on these grounds, the bishop shall first notify the incumbent of his concerns in writing and shall afford the incumbent a reasonable time to respond and, where appropriate, to take remedial action.

8. Where a permission granted under paragraph 4 is in force, the incumbent shall not admit any child to Holy Communion unless he or she is satisfied that (a) the child has been baptised and (b) a person having parental responsibility for the child is content that the child should be so admitted. Otherwise, subject to any direction of the bishop, it is within the incumbent's absolute discretion to decide whether, and if so when, any child should first be admitted to Holy Communion.

9. The incumbent shall maintain a register of all children admitted to Holy Communion under these Regulations, and where practicable will record on the child's baptismal certificate the date and place of the child's first admission. If the baptismal certificate is not available, the incumbent shall present the child with a separate certificate recording the same details.

10. A child who presents evidence in the form stipulated in paragraph 9 that he or she has been admitted to Holy Communion under these Regulations shall be so admitted at any service of Holy Communion conducted according to the rites of the Church of

England in any place, regardless of whether or not any permission under paragraph 4 is in force in that place or was in force in that place until revoked.

11. These Regulations shall apply to a cathedral as if it were a parish, with the modifications that:

    (a) any application under paragraphs 3 or 7 must be made by the dean of the cathedral concerned, accompanied by a copy of a resolution in support of the application passed by the chapter of the cathedral concerned;

    (b) the obligations imposed on the incumbent under paragraphs 8 and 9 shall be imposed on the dean of the cathedral concerned.

12. A diocesan bishop may delegate any of his functions under these Regulations (except his functions under paragraph 3) to a person appointed by him for the purpose, being a suffragan or assistant bishop or archdeacon of the diocese.

13. In these Regulations:

    (a) 'incumbent', in relation to a parish, includes:

        (i) in a case where the benefice concerned is vacant (and paragraph (ii) below does not apply), the rural dean;

        (ii) in a case where a suspension period (within the meaning of the Pastoral Measure 1983) applies to the benefice concerned, the priest-in-charge; and

        (iii) in a case where a special cure of souls in respect of the parish has been assigned to a vicar in a team ministry by a Scheme under the Pastoral Measure 1983 or by licence from the bishop, that vicar; and

    (b) references to paragraph numbers are to the relevant paragraph or paragraphs in these Regulations.

Appendix 2
A review of resource material

Nothing is so easily out of date than a review of resource material, yet no encouraging book is complete without such a section. The development of children and communion is an on-going learning process for the Church, and any self-respecting parish should invest in good resources and keep up to date with new material.

Resource material to get you started

Diana Craven and Mark Stafford (eds), *About to Receive: Resources for Exploring the Eucharist* (Diocese of Southwark, 2005)
> A staggeringly beautiful and useful book produced by a number of practitioners for all ages and levels of understanding. This vast resource book is good for groups, congregations and preaching inspiration.

Leslie J. Francis and Jeff Astley, *Children, Churches and Christian Learning* (SPCK, 2002).
> This book encompasses every aspect of children's work. Every parish should have a copy. This is all about good practice.

Leslie J. Francis and Diane Drayson, *His Spirit Is with Us: A Project-based Programme on Communion* (Kevin Mayhew, 2003).
> A programme of education and learning to go with an illustrated communion book also by Leslie Francis.

Nick Harding, *Share: A Communion Preparation Course for 7–11s* (Kevin Mayhew, 2002).
> Nick is the pro-active Children's Officer in the Diocese of Southwell and Nottingham. This is a course for 7 to 11s and has two useful sessions for parents.

Daphne Kirk, *When a Child Asks to Take Communion* (Kevin Mayhew, 2003).
> A useful little book to hand to parents.

Diana Murrie, *My Baptism Book: A Child's Guide to Baptism* (Church House Publishing, 2006).
It doesn't get better than this. The Church must give these away to those baptized.

Diana Murrie, *My Communion Book: A Child's Guide to Holy Communion* (Church House Publishing, 2002).

Diana Murrie, *The Baptism Cube* (Church House Publishing, 2006).
A vital addition to *The Communion Cube* (see below) and with even better artwork. It is supplemented by the excellent companion book, *My Baptism Book* (see above).

Diana Murrie and Steve Pearce, *Children and Holy Communion* (Kevin Mayhew, 2003).
Originally published by Church House Publishing, this was the book that started it all off in the Church of England. This is a structure book, good as a summary to help you build your programme. Again, every parish needs a copy.

Diana Murrie and Margaret Withers, *The Communion Cube* (Church House Publishing, 2002).
The ecclesiastical answer to Rubik's Cube, and enjoyed as much by adults in dull sermons as by children. Every 'busy bag' should have one of these or *The Baptism Cube* (see above). *The Communion Cube* is supported by *My Communion Book* (see above).

Peter Reiss, *Children and Communion: A Practical Guide for Interested Churches* (Grove Books, 1998).
Though out of date now, this is a useful summary. It is good if you can't be bothered to read my book.

Susan Sayers, *Bread and Wine People: An All-age On-going Parish Training Programme for Full Participation in the Eucharist* (Kevin Mayhew, 2001).
Susan's familiar style is friendly and helpful. This photocopiable resource provides a number of teaching Eucharists.

Aileen Urquhart, *I Belong – Common Worship: First Holy Communion Programme* (Redemptorist Publications, 2001).
A colourful course, now somewhat out of date but a good resource to have on the shelf, especially the Parents' Guide and the Teachers' Guide.

Hans Urs Von Balthasar, *Unless You Become Like This Child* (Ignatius Press, 1991).

The best little book you can read about the theology of children in the Bible.

Margaret Withers, *Mission-shaped Children: Moving towards a Child-centred Church* (Church House Publishing, 2006).

Margaret places children at the centre of the mission-shaped agenda. This is essential reading for every parish. While not specifically about children and communion, the need for engagement comes through in every breath. 'The insights in this book will help the Church regain both hope and vision for its mission among children' (The Revd Jackie Cray and Bishop Graham Cray in the Foreword).

Margaret Withers, *Welcome to the Lord's Table: A Practical Course for Preparing Children to Receive Holy Communion* (Barnabas, 2006).

This is a revision of Margaret Withers' book, *Welcome to the Lord's Table*, first published in 1998. If there is one preparation course that is the set text, this is it. This is a journey book with as much helpful information and sound teaching as any parish of any complexion could need. There is an additional activity book, also by Margaret Withers (*Welcome to the Lord's Table: Activity Book*, published by Barnabas, 1999), which can be used in conjunction with the course or as a stand-alone handbook for each child. No one who reads *Let the Children Come . . . to Communion* should be without these two books.

Service booklets

Leslie J. Francis, *The Lord is Here! An Illustrated Communion Book for Common Worship* (Kevin Mayhew, 2003).

Susan Sayers, *Jesus Is Here: Children's Communion Book* (Kevin Mayhew, 1993).

SPCK, *I can join in Common Worship* (2003).

Aileen Urquhart, *My Holy Communion Book: Order One* (Redemptorist Publications, 2001).

With wipe clean pages!

Other resource books

Joan Brown, *Celebrating with Children: Liturgical Celebrations for Children Preparing for the Sacraments of Reconciliation and Eucharist* (Kevin Mayhew, 1999).

Sofia Cavalletti, *The Religious Potential of the Child: 6 to 12 Year Old (Catechesis of the Good Shepherd Publications)* (Liturgy Training Publications, 2002).
A catechetical approach to Montessori learning for children.

Donald Hilton, *Table Talk: Looking at the Communion Meal from the Outside and the Inside* (United Reformed Church, 1998).
Reflections on the Eucharist with the participation of children.

Paddy Rylands, *Journey Together towards First Holy Communion: Resources for Catechists Accompanying Parents of Children Preparing to Celebrate First Holy Communion* (Kevin Mayhew, 2000).

Victoria M. Tufano (ed.), *Readings in the Christian Initiation of Children* (Liturgy Training Publications, 1994).
Not what the title says, but a series of thoughtful essays.

Mark Water, *What God Has To Say About Children* (John Hunt Publishing, 2003).
A gift book with lots of useful biblical references.

Website

www.cofe.anglican.org

Appendix 3
Wendy's story

When I heard that our parish was to take part in admitting small children to Holy Communion, my immediate reaction was one of shock and total disbelief. I wasn't prepared for the intensity of my feelings and I was surprised and bewildered.

I spent a sleepless night: thinking, praying and mulling it over. The Church had, I decided, lost direction. In the morning, I poured it all out in a letter to Fr Stephen. I was one of those people who believed that, in order to take this sacrament, it was necessary to be able to acknowledge the concept of sin and the need for forgiveness, so that reconcilement to God was an ongoing act; it was necessary to understand, in some measure, the redemptive work of Christ on the cross.

But I also believe that Christ loves children and that they hold a very special place in his heart. To this end, they already belonged to him and it was unnecessary for them to take this sacrament until they became streetwise and, therefore, able and willing to seek his forgiveness. I also said to Fr Stephen that perhaps if I knew the thinking behind this astonishing move, I would understand and feel differently about things.

Fr Stephen replied with concern and suggested we talk it over. He said that he wouldn't try to persuade me, but that there were detailed historical and theological issues which I would want to know.

Remaining sceptical, I began reading the very early history of the Church alongside the Bible. It was fascinating, but it didn't convince me. I also read twelfth-century literature up to the Reformation, when Cranmer and so many others were burnt at the stake for not being able to say they believed in transubstantiation. I began to go off the Church in a big way and grew more and more unhappy. The services passed in a blur and I couldn't seem to be in touch with anything. I told the family I was thinking of joining the Quakers.

My prayers pleaded that the bishops would see their error in leading the people of God astray or, if it were the right way to be going, that this way would be shown to me. Fr Stephen didn't try to persuade me; at first I was glad but months later, when I felt I was drowning and exhausted from the emotion of it all, I wanted to scream at him to come and prove it then.

God moves in mysterious ways.

I went along to the service before our PCC meeting one Thursday evening. I needed some quiet and peace – it had been one of those fraught days. I knelt at the back in the Lady Chapel. Fr Stephen came to sit beside me; we stood for the Gospel reading, which was from Mark, chapter 9. I don't remember all the verses, but I shall never forget these. The curate Fr Henry read:

> Then he took a little child and put it among them – and taking it in his arms, he said to them, 'Whoever welcomes one such child in my name welcomes me and whoever welcomes me, welcomes not me, but the one who sent me. If any of you put a stumbling block before one of these little ones who believe in me, it would be better for you if a great millstone were hung around your neck and you were thrown into the sea.'

It was as if this Gospel was speaking just to me that evening. I felt got at. Soon I was back on my knees saying: 'Depart from me, Lord, for I am sinful.' I also felt very afraid because if he departed, what then? I'm glad to say he didn't depart, although the struggle was far from over.

Fr Stephen came back to his place and, when it was time to go for Communion, he stood to let me out but I wasn't going anywhere. After a moment, he knelt too and didn't receive Communion that evening. Christ had taken me by the hand.

That was the turning point but, I told myself, I was holding to the teaching of the Church as I had received it for almost 60 years – and now it was all wrong.

I asked myself four questions and answered them.

1. Why do I go to church?	To worship God
2. Is this fundamental to my faith that Jesus Christ is the Son of God?	No
3. Am I more worthy than anyone else to receive the sacrament?	No
4. Could I cope with not going to church?	No

My conscience now was a bother and I came to church with a very heavy heart. 'Show me the way, Lord' was my constant prayer.

A subsequent step came after a chance remark to a member of our ministry team; she asked if I would like to talk about it. She really listened and when someone does that you actually hear yourself. The agony of the crucifixion has always been paramount to me, especially the point at which Jesus is nailed to the cross, and I suppose I thought that everyone would feel this. I was concerned for the children in that respect, too, because for me the Eucharist brings a re-enactment of that horrible death. I thought Christ would want to shield them from that but, at the same time, I thought it was right that people receiving did feel it. Gently, I was helped to see that everyone received in a different way and that Christ comes to each person uniquely. With that realization came the feeling that a great weight was being lifted off me, but there was still a lingering hesitation.

The third step was when Fr Stephen suggested I attend the conference at Salisbury. It was a privilege to be a part of that. In an open discussion at the conference, the bishop said that God's love for his children does not depend on age or knowledge or understanding. He loves continually on our journey to him. This journey begins at baptism.

How could I resist any further? But, as if I needed further confirmation that this was the way ahead, on the last page of my favourite spiritual book *The Imitation of Christ*, written in the fifteenth century by Thomas à Kempis, it says:

> Man should not be a curious searcher into this sacrament, but a humble follower of Christ. God walketh with the simple, revealeth himself to the humble and giveth understanding to little ones. He hideth his grace from the curious and proud.

To sum all this up, Julian of Norwich has had the last word:

> I was answered in inward understanding, saying,

> Would you know your Lord's meaning in this? Learn it well, Love was his meaning. Who showed it you? Love. Why did he show you? For love. Hold fast to this, and you shall learn and know more about love, but you will never need to know or understand about anything else for ever and ever.

Lightning Source UK Ltd.
Milton Keynes UK
UKHW021037201218
334311UK00006B/199/P